CARIBBEAN TRADE, INTEGRATION AND DEVELOPMENT

CARIBBEAN TRADE, INTEGRATION AND DEVELOPMENT

Selected Papers and Speeches of Alister McIntyre

VOLUME 2: ASPECTS OF HUMAN RESOURCES
DEVELOPMENT AND HIGHER EDUCATION

EDITED BY

Andrew S. Downes, Compton Bourne,
M. Arnold McIntyre and Rosalie O'Meally

Canoe Press

Jamaica • Barbados • Trinidad and Tobago

Canoe Press

The University of the West Indies Press
7A Gibraltar Hall Road, Mona
Kingston 7, Jamaica
www.uwipress.com

ISBN: 978-976-653-036-5 (print)
978-976-653-037-2 (ePub)

A catalogue record of this book is available from the National Library of Jamaica.

Printed in the United States of America

Dedication

To past and current generations of Caribbean economists who have devoted their attention to the intellectual foundations of Caribbean integration and development. Their ideas and activities have provided the groundwork for the development of institutions and policies upon which future generations of economists can build.

Contents

Section 1 Human Resources Development in Small Developing Countries

Section 2   The Role of the University in the Development Process

Figures

Tables

About the Editors

Andrew S. Downes
Professor Emeritus of Economics,
Former Pro Vice Chancellor (Planning and Development) and
Director, Sir Arthur Lewis Institute of Social and Economic Studies,
The University of the West Indies.

Compton Bourne
Professor Emeritus of Economics,
The University of the West Indies.
Former President, Caribbean Development Bank,
Former Campus Principal (St Augustine) and Pro Vice Chancellor,
The University of the West Indies.

M. Arnold McIntyre
Deputy Division Chief, Western Hemisphere Department,
International Monetary Fund.
Former Trade Analyst and Policy Advisor at the following regional institutions:
Caribbean Development Bank, Organization of Eastern Caribbean States,
CARICOM Export Development Agency and the Caribbean Regional
Negotiation Machinery (now designated the Office of Trade Negotiations,
CARICOM).

Rosalie O'Meally
Former Director, Office of the Vice Chancellor,
The University of the West Indies.
Former Project Director,
Caribbean Regional Negotiating Machinery.

Tribute

Sir Shridath Ramphal GCMG, AC, ONZ, OE, OCC, QC

This is intended as a tribute to Sir Alister McIntyre, but as I approach the delightful task, I acknowledge its essential shortcomings. For what better tribute can be paid to Sir Alister than this collection itself. Those persons responsible for offering to posterity his ideas and ideals, his technical skills and counsel, his wisdom and practicality through his writings over a lifetime of service are paying the best tribute of all. This collection is the ultimate memorial to Alister McIntyre, and I am proud to identify with it in this modest way.

When I read Alister's 2016 reflections – *The Caribbean and the Wider World* – I knew that those ruminations on his life and career were the alluvial gems and that mining the gold beneath lay ahead. The team responsible for publishing this collection of his papers in these two volumes has fulfilled that promise. He would have wished it so, and the great credit must go to the team comprising Andrew, Arnold, Compton and Rosalie, who undertook the main task, for the treasure they have brought forth. The "McIntyre Papers" will occupy an honoured place in West Indian historiography.

Alister was four years younger than me when we met in his early days at the Institute of Social and Economic Research (ISER), Mona. It was the 1950s, and he had just completed his courses at the London School of Economics and Oxford University, while I was grappling with "federal" hopes and lapses in Port of Spain. We were two young West Indians in an orbit that would last all our lives.

The papers in these volumes inevitably chart the course of Sir Alister's professional life, and as I marvel at the prodigious output of his intellectual journey, I recall the innumerable paths we travelled in tandem and I am filled with a sense of thankfulness for our walking together on so many of them.

The 1950s saw the rise and fall of our hopes for West Indian federalism, but neither Alister nor I lost faith in a Caribbean destiny of unity within our regional space. We both saw *West Indianness* within the wider context of the developing world and of a global domain which had to accommodate an inseparable humanity.

The decade that followed saw the unfolding of our dreams beyond federalism with the conception of the Caribbean Free Trade Association (CARIFTA) in Antigua in 1965 and its birth at Chaguaramas: namely, the first Treaty of Chaguaramas in 1973 as CARIFTA began. We started the necessary movement from CARIFTA to the Caribbean Community (CARICOM) and to the still unattained goals of the CARICOM Single Market and Economy (CSME).

They were years of insistent yearning and striving, and Alister McIntyre was never far from these developments, as his papers reveal. With his intellectual twin, William Demas, he provided the technical underpinnings of regional integration beyond the political crawl that persistently defied their full counsel.

I welcomed Alister to Georgetown in 1974 as CARICOM secretary-general – he and his illustrious family. That position placed him at the centre of Caribbean development; and his strengths helped every effort from the Grand Anse Declaration, the West Indian Commission's *Time for Action*, to the *Organization of Eastern Caribbean States* (*OECS*) and the widening and deepening of CARICOM and the Caribbean Regional Negotiating Machinery (CRNM). He later led the University of the West Indies as Vice Chancellor in the orbit with me as Chancellor. Sir Alister's talents reached out beyond his Caribbean homeland. In 1975, when I was elected Secretary-General of the Commonwealth Secretariat, the Heads of Commonwealth Governments named Alister McIntyre to head an illustrious panel of Commonwealth Experts on the New International Economic Order. Their report would command global attention. In addition, he served the cause of development directly at the United Nations Conference on Trade and Development (UNCTAD).

Sir John Mordecai ended his priceless account of the "federal negotiations" with some words of questioning by Sir Arthur Lewis on the failure of the federal experiment despite the high quality of the Manley-Williams-Adams triumvirate. Perhaps future generations guided by these papers will ask why – with the technical excellence of Sir Alister McIntyre on hand, and the generation of economists he guided – has West Indian political leadership failed to fulfil its dreams and promises of true West Indian unity?

June 30, 2021

Foreword

Alister McIntyre, OCC, OM, CCH, has been described variously as economic consultant, economic advisor, scholar and policymaker. Perhaps, the most insightful characterization is the one provided by the Honourable Lloyd Best in 1998, entitled "Sir Alister McIntyre, Polycrat and Nation Builder". The papers in this collection support that designation.

One of the central features of this collection is the focus on building a Caribbean sustainable space through regional integration for successful international trade negotiations and a trading system that promotes development.

What distinguished McIntyre from many of his colleagues was not only the technical brilliance of his writings on trade and economics but his equally perceptive understanding of the role of human resources in the building of a sustainable livelihood in small developing states. These papers reflect the vision of one who was committed to creating an economic space to facilitate the movement of economic factors, goods, services, skills and human resources. They underscore Best's view that Sir Alister was a nation builder. But the nation he envisaged was not the individual territories in the Caribbean space; instead, the one he proposed, advocated, participated in and informed the building of those institutions that would collectively constitute the Caribbean nation, as he conceived it.

Sir Alister's deep interests such as human resource development, education, training and the capacity to deal with the challenges of change in the twenty-first century are all deftly addressed in his many contributions to scholarship. West Indian nationhood was for him something not only to be desired but to work for tirelessly, and as many of these papers indicate, he spent much of his life in the commitment to public service which provided the appropriate fora through which he demonstrated the vital leadership required to support those institutions and policies needed to anchor the Caribbean nation as a vital component of sustainable growth in the region with the capacity to manage its relationship with the outside world.

The importance of these papers is that they have captured and documented the experiences of the author and the means by which he influenced and inspired generations of Caribbean people. The positions of trust that he held in the region and internationally, including Secretary-General of the Caribbean Community (CARICOM); Director of United Nations Conference of Trade and Services (UNCTAD); Under Secretary of the United Nations; Vice Chancellor of the University of the West Indies (UWI); and Chief Technical Director of the Caribbean Regional Negotiating Machinery (CRNM), would have all placed him in the unique position to access the needs of the region and to mobilize the resources needed to underpin its development imperatives. These papers are therefore significant in that they represent the body of ideas and policy direction of a leader who held these positions. It is in this sense that the selected papers demonstrate that he was not simply an administrator, but he brought to these positions leadership in ideas which he shared through his writings.

As one who has been influenced by his ideas and who has benefited by association with him in the various positions in the region, I must commend the editors for preserving the legacy of this iconic Caribbean patriot and for making available to future generations, scholars and policymakers a viable model of what can and should be done in order to empower this Caribbean region with the critical capacity to respond and reflect the aspirations of the Caribbean people.

The Most Honourable Professor Sir Kenneth Octavius Hall, ON, GCMG, OJ

May 27, 2021

Acknowledgements

The editors would like to thank Sir Alister McIntyre for agreeing to undertake this project. After reading his autobiography entitled *The Caribbean and the Wider World: Commentaries on My Life and Career*, the editors thought that several of his papers and speeches required a wider audience since many of his ideas and analyses are relevant to trade, integration and development issues facing the contemporary Caribbean.

The former General Manager of the UWI Press, Dr Joseph Powell, recently passed, and his staff, especially Nadine Buckland, Althea Brown, Shivaun Hearne and Donna Muirhead along with consultant Mohammed Raffi offered excellent advice and assistance in the preparation of the collection. Beverley Hinds, Librarian in the Audine Wilkinson Library at the Cave Hill Campus of the Sir Arthur Lewis Institute of Social and Economic Studies (SALISES), supplied some of the papers contained in this collection. Mrs Bernadette Worrell-Johnson, Librarian, West Indies and Special Collections, Main Library, UWI, Mona Campus, and Mrs Thelma White, Librarian, Sir Arthur Lewis Institute for Social and Economic Studies, UWI, Mona Campus, have also been extremely helpful in sourcing and accessing Sir Alister's early works.

Dr Angela Ramsay and her team must be given very special thanks for providing superb professional editing services, which have greatly enhanced the quality of the publication. We also acknowledge the timely assistance rendered by the Vice Chancellor of the UWI, Sir Hilary Beckles, and the Chairpersons of the Board of Directors of the UWI Press, Dr Luz Longsworth and Professor Densil Williams, in facilitating the production of the volumes.

Several organizations should be thanked for releasing the copyright for a number of the articles and monographs published by Sir Alister. These organizations include the C. D. Howe Institute, Sir Arthur Lewis Institute of Social and Economic Studies, the University of the West Indies, Central Bank of Trinidad and Tobago, Commonwealth Secretariat, the Gleaner Co Ltd, the Grace Kennedy Foundation, the West India Committee, the United Nations, Institute of Development Studies, University of Sussex, University of Puerto Rico, Royal Society of Arts, Institute of Latin American Studies, University of London, Caribbean Development Bank and the Inter-American Development Bank.

We would like to offer our sincere thanks to three organizations for their generous financial contributions which made this publication possible: the International Development Research Centre (IDRC), the Caribbean Development Bank (CDB) and the ANSA McAL Foundation. We acknowledge the assistance of key persons in these organizations for facilitating the arrangements: Lucy Gray-Donald and Federico Burone of the IDRC, Dr Warren Smith and Volville Forsythe of the CDB, and Maria Superville-Neilson of the ANSA McAL Foundation.

We acknowledge the permission of the International Monetary Fund for allowing one of the editors to participate in this project. Marjorie McIntyre provided the moral and loving support expected of a spouse during the preparation of the text.

Alister McIntyre participated fully in the selection of the papers included in these two volumes and also commented on the introductory commentaries prepared by the editors. He passed away on April 20, 2019, in Jamaica at age eighty-seven.

The papers and speeches in these volumes reflect his lasting contribution and legacy to Caribbean economic development.

Introduction

Sir Alister McIntyre is regarded as one of the Caribbean's most distinguished and respected economists. He was the Director of the Institute of Social and Economic Research (ISER) and the Vice Chancellor of the University of the West Indies (UWI). He taught economics in the Department of Economics at the Mona and St Augustine campuses of the university. He was also the Secretary-General of the Caribbean Community (CARICOM) Secretariat, Director of Commodities and Deputy Secretary-General of United Nations Conference on Trade and Development (UNCTAD), in addition to being the Chief Technical Advisor at the Caribbean Regional Negotiating Machinery (CRNM).

Alister McIntyre has made an enormous and lasting contribution to Caribbean economic policymaking and analysis. He was at the forefront of key economic decisions on the economic integration process in the Caribbean, international trading negotiations involving African, Caribbean and Pacific Countries (ACP) and Europe, and a pioneer in the development of the human resources base of the Caribbean region, especially through UWI. His autobiography, entitled *The Caribbean and the Wider World: Commentaries on My Life and Career*, mentions several important papers that he had written over his illustrious career as academic economist, regional and international technocrat, university administrator and trade negotiator. Though several of these papers are not readily accessible, this collection should provide readers with an understanding of the enormous value of his papers and speeches.

The collection provides economists, development and trade analysts a window into his keen insight on trade, economic integration and development issues facing the Caribbean region. The papers illustrate the depth of his understanding of the economic and trading challenges facing the region since the 1960s. Although some of the papers were written in that decade, a close reading will indicate that many of the issues and challenges identified by McIntyre at that time are still realities today. Indeed, the collection provides the "grist to the mill" for several of today's trade and development issues facing the region. Many economists and students who tend to ignore the historical context of development issues should find his writings to be a lucid and pertinent analysis of today's issues.

The collection is divided into two volumes, with three sections in volume 1 and two sections in volume 2. Each section contains an introductory commentary by the editors which places the chapters in context and updates issues arising from the chapters.

In volume 1, section 1 examines the regional economic integration experience in the Caribbean. Since the early 1970s, the nations within the region have been engaged in the challenging process of establishing an economic integration movement. McIntyre played a seminal role in this process as the secretary-general of the Caribbean Community Secretariat and a senior member of the University of the West Indies

(UWI). Given the slow pace of the economic integration movement in the region, the papers and speeches in this section provide insights into the process of establishing a single market and economy.

Section 2 provides a perspective on international trading relations and negotiations in a dynamic and competitive global economy. The articles provide vital lessons for persons involved in negotiating trade agreements between Caribbean countries and other countries and regions. A key lesson derived from his experience as an international bureaucrat and negotiator is that Caribbean persons engaged in international trading and negotiations should be thoroughly prepared and up to date on international economic and political events and trends.

Section 3 discusses the trends and challenges associated with the future of Caribbean trade and development. McIntyre is of the view that the region ought to adopt a strategic approach to trade and development issues that aligns with the reality of small developing states and that the region should take greater advantage of the opportunities offered by the global economy, especially key trading partners.

In volume 2, section 1 covers a salient aspect of McIntyre's lifework, namely human resources development in the Caribbean region. He recognized that the future of Caribbean development and an improved standard of living of Caribbean nationals lie in knowledge and skill investment and that a knowledgeable and skilled workforce was the key to fostering economic diversification and growth in the region. He also emphasized the development of knowledge economies which can compete effectively in the global economy.

Section 2 examines the UWI as a case study in the human resources development of the region, particularly in the creation of "knowledge economies". As Vice Chancellor of the University, he argued that the UWI should play a central role in the development of knowledge economies. He, however, acknowledged the challenges constraining the UWI's role to contribute fully to this development. The chapters in this section serve as a useful complement to the chapters in section 1 and would be valuable required reading for university administrators.

Since the papers and speeches in this collection were prepared over the period 1964 to 2008, it is noteworthy that Alister McIntyre provides an epilogue on the future of trade, investment and development in the region.

A list of his addresses, lectures, speeches and papers is provided at the end of the Epilogue.

This collection will primarily be useful to economists with an interest in trade policy, economic integration and development, in addition to public policy analysts and trade negotiators. University planners and educators will also find that the collection could add significant meaning and context to their work. Students taking courses in development studies and trade policy will also find the collection to be most informative and instructive.

Abbreviations

ACP	African, Caribbean and Pacific States
ACTI	Association of Caribbean Tertiary Institutions
CAIC	Caribbean Association of Industry and Commerce
CARICOM	Caribbean Community
CARIFTA	Caribbean Free Trade Association
CARNEID	Caribbean Network of Educational Innovation for Development
CAST	College of Arts, Science and Technology
CDB	Caribbean Development Bank
CGDS	Centre for Gender and Development Studies
CIDA	Canadian International Development Agency
CRNM	Caribbean Regional Negotiating Machinery
CSME	CARICOM Single Market and Economy
CXC	Caribbean Examination Council
ECLAC	Economic Commission for Latin America and the Caribbean
EDF	European Development Fund
EEC	European Economic Community
EMBA	Executive Master of Business Administration
FAO	Food and Agriculture Organization
FTAA	Free Trade Agreement of the Americas
GDP	Gross domestic product
GNP	Gross national product
HRD	Human resources development
IADB	Inter-American Development Bank
IDRC	International Development Research Centre
IMF	International Monetary Fund
ISER	Institute of Social and Economic Research
LAFTA	Latin American Free Trade Association
MBA	Master of Business Administration
NISTEP	National In-service Teacher Programme
OAS	Organization of American States
OCOD	Organization for Cooperation in Overseas Development
OECD	Organization for Economic Cooperation and Development
OECS	Organization of Eastern Caribbean States
PPP	Private-public sector partnership
R&D	Research and development
S&T	Science and technology
SALISES	Sir Arthur Lewis Institute of Social and Economic Studies
SDC	Small developing countries

STEM	Science, Technology, Engineering and Mathematics
TMRU	Tropical Metabolism Research Unit
TPP	Trans-Pacific Partnership
UG	University of Guyana
UNCTAD	United Nations Conference on Trade and Development
UNDP	United Nations Development Programme
UNESCO	United Nations Educational, Scientific and Cultural Organization
UNICEF	United Nations Children's Fund
USAID	United States Agency for International Development
UWIDITE	University of the West Indies Distance Teaching Experiment
UWI	University of the West Indies
WIGUT	West Indies Group of University Teachers
WTO	World Trade Organization
YTEPP	Youth Training and Employment Partnership Programme

Section 1

Human Resources Development in Small
Developing Countries

Introduction to Section 1

The term "human resources" refers to the knowledge, skills, talents, energies and competencies of persons that can be harnessed for the production of goods and services. As Harbison (1973, p.3) has stated, human resources "constitute the ultimate basis for the wealth of nations. Capital and natural resources are passive factors of production; human beings are the active agents who accumulate capital, exploit natural resources, build social, economic and political organisations, and carry forward national development". The term "human resources development" (HRD) refers to the set of systematic and planned activities, programmes and projects designed to increase the quantity and quality of the human resources available to an economic unit (that is, a firm, industry, nation or region). HRD has far-reaching implications not only for the production of goods and services but also for an individual's self-development.

Human resource development has a multiplicity of interconnecting dimensions, including educational attainment levels, the quality and relevance of the education, workforce competencies and the physical and mental health of the population: HRD also incorporates employment policies that allow businesses to thrive, with export business being the emphasis in these papers. In this context, HRD embraces not only the production of goods and provision of services but also the quality of life of the population, including the reduction of crime and violence that has plagued some of the small island states of the Caribbean.

HRD is the instrument that creates the momentum for economic development. Low human resource development is addressed through coherent policies, strategies that are mindful of policy linkages and a nation's capacity for planning, implementation and evaluation.

Human resources development is an integral theme in McIntyre's work, particularly in the areas of education and training. He notes that in small developing countries (SDCs) with limited natural resources, HRD plays a critical role in economic growth and national development. In the nine papers on this subject, he links HRD to the development of the knowledge economy, the information age, productivity growth and the reduction of unemployment in the Caribbean region. Indeed, as stated in the previous sections on international trade and economic integration, the enhanced competitiveness of production is vital to export growth of the region, and HRD plays a special role in promoting international competitiveness especially through productivity growth.

In his paper "Human Resources Development: Its Relevance to Jamaica and the Caribbean", McIntyre expands on the links between HRD, the knowledge revolution, research and development, technological developments, productivity and improvements in socio-economic welfare. He points to the pivotal role of service exports in the growth and development of the Caribbean. He also expands upon the increasing power of information and communications technology in the global economy on competitive consumer and producer services. He notes the emergence of new technologies in several fields, not limited to biotechnology, information technology and material sciences, artificial intelligence, and robotics. Given the challenges associated with the expansion of traditional sectors such as agriculture, manufacturing, mining and services, he argues for the use of the knowledge revolution to revitalize these sectors and develop new sectors such as financial and cultural sectors, especially for the export market. He explores HRD's enabling role in providing the inputs needed to realize the development of these sectors.

In a series of papers on the education and training system within the Caribbean, McIntyre points to the several deficiencies that have constrained the development process within the region. The deficiencies result in the relatively low levels of economic growth that have led to poverty and income inequality, youth unemployment and limited product diversification. He highlights the low levels of enrolment and attainment in secondary schools, a serious shortfall at the tertiary level, limited opportunities for acquiring technical and industrial skills and the unsatisfactory levels of enrolment in Science, Technology, Engineering and Mathematics fields. He expresses his concern about the limited investment and involvement in research and development (R&D), which can be commercialized, and the inadequate investments in teacher training and educational infrastructure. Although improvements have occurred in some of these areas since the early 1990s when McIntyre wrote about them, they remain pressing concerns for the region. As he notes: "the principal problem in primary and secondary [education] has been one of *quality rather than quantity*'. In the case of the tertiary system, serious deficiencies are evident in quantity and, in some cases, the quality of education". Indeed "the principal problem at the tertiary level is one of *access*". In this regard, University of the West Indies (UWI)'s strategic plan 2017 to 2022 has "Access" as one of its themes. Linking HRD to economic development, he argues that "economic development requires a significant expansion in the number of tertiary graduates" and persons with technical expertise. He emphasizes that the Caribbean region lags behind the rest of the world in the production of tertiary-level graduates and the urgent need to expand enrolment and graduation rates to meet the demands of the labour market in the region.

In short, he underscores the necessity of educational reform in the Caribbean to meet the human resource needs of the new economic era, increasingly being referred to as the fourth industrial revolution or 4IR. Given the inter-relatedness of the different levels of the educational system, he argues that a strategic approach is required to achieve educational reform from the early childhood level to the tertiary level. Since this reform would require significant financial resources, McIntyre recommends that key stakeholders, such as the Caribbean Development Bank (CDB), the Inter-American Development Bank (IADB), the World Bank and other financial institutions, partner with governments to provide resources for infrastructural development, equipment, curriculum development training and the creation and production of excellent teaching materials. The private sector should also become a major partner in educational reform by participating in cost-sharing arrangements, as the public purse cannot meet the demands of the educational system.

McIntyre notes that "free education at the secondary and tertiary levels is no longer feasible" without "a deterioration in standards". Hence policymakers should hold discussions to arrive at the "best" methods of funding education in fiscally constrained countries considering the rising costs of education. McIntyre proposes a model which includes "free" (publicly provided) primary education and partially funded secondary and tertiary education with the proviso that the ability to pay should be a major consideration. Indeed, several Caribbean countries have introduced universal publicly funded primary and secondary level education and have gradually moved to cost-sharing arrangements at the tertiary level with loan funding schemes.

McIntyre offers several suggestions for improving education and training. Some of the suggestions have been implemented at varying levels in the region. Illustrations of the implemented recommendations in education are distance and online delivery of programmes, the promotion of technical and vocational education, the adoption of remedial programmes in areas such as mathematics and technology, the promotion of STEM areas, especially in the secondary and tertiary educational levels; curriculum development with the help of the Caribbean Examinations Council (CXC); inter-institutional linkages and more teacher training opportunities. Other recommendations implemented are private-public sector partnerships (PPP), and cost recovery methods of financing, the adoption of cost-effective methods, the promotion of entrepreneurship and apprenticeships.

He implores educational institutions to help themselves by developing "new sources of dynamism and innovation". UWI, for example, has sought to follow this recommendation through its strategic plans.

A major issue facing the region and highlighted by McIntyre is the non-existence or paucity of data on several important dimensions of the human resource problem. The development of a comprehensive human resources information system is critical to HRD in the region. He laments the weak data relating to the labour market and educational and training outputs in the various countries, which thwarts human resource development, a problem still existing today.

Furthermore, progress with productivity improvement cannot be tracked without the requisite data. As previously indicated, HRD promotes productivity which in turn enhances international competitiveness and export expansion. McIntyre notes a decline in productivity in the traditional sectors of the region; hence efforts should be made to improve total productivity in the new and revitalized sectors. He argues for the urgent establishment of a science and technology capacity, a greater research and development effort in tertiary institutions, increased private sector activism and investment in innovation and entrepreneurship, more private-public sector partnerships in knowledge-based sectors, macroeconomic stability and the negotiation of productivity agreements between labour unions and employers, initiatives which are driven in large part by HRD.

The development of the knowledge economy and the associated developments in the human resources of the region play a vital role in McIntyre's vision for the "new Caribbean economy". He envisions tertiary institutions such as UWI, playing a strategic role in this new economy. As the World Bank (2007) indicates, two of the pillars of the knowledge economy include the education and training base of the country (that is, an educated and skilled labour force) and the innovation system (that is, the research centres and tertiary-level education, which engage in new knowledge creation, transfer and application). In the context of the Caribbean, the elements of the knowledge economy are still missing. Indeed, the World Economic Forum's report on the region points to only Trinidad and Tobago being in the "innovation stage of development". While other regional nations are transitioning to the innovation stage, greater efforts are needed to create the economic environment that allows the required leap. McIntyre makes the case for fast-tracking the process via HRD by creating greater access to higher education, especially in the areas of science and technology, with UWI taking the lead. This approach would provide the region with the expertise to promote new exports especially in the services sectors and take advantage of the various provisions in trade agreements. As he states, trade in new areas of production will be the driver for skilled human resources in the region.

The papers in this section are of great value as they outline the elements of an HRD strategy for the Caribbean region that would complement the trade and integration strategy discussed in the previous sections in volume 1. The papers demonstrate the relevance of McIntyre's ideas to the development of the Caribbean region as the challenges he identifies still face the region, and his suggestions for overcoming the challenges are most pertinent to current development thinking.

References

Harbison F.H. (1973): *Human Resources as the Wealth of Nations* (New York, Oxford University Press).

World Bank (2007): *Building Knowledge Economies: Advanced Strategies for Development* (Washington, DC).

Chapter 1.1

Human Resources Development

Its Relevance to Jamaica and the Caribbean: Second
Grace Kennedy Foundation Lecture, Kingston,
Jamaica, 1990

The Concept of Human Resources Development and the Knowledge Revolution

I am very pleased to be the second speaker in the Grace Kennedy Foundation Lecture series. It is a tall order to follow the Honourable G. Arthur Brown, whose lectures were a model of specialized knowledge and clarity of expression. I shall speak on human resources development, which picks up some of the themes emphasized in the first lecture and expands on issues of relevance to Jamaica and the Caribbean.

The Two Dimensions of Human Resources Development

There are two dimensions to human resources development. One dimension is concerned with the contribution that human beings make to the production of goods and provision of services by applying human effort and ingenuity to a country's endowments of natural resources, technology and capital equipment. Indeed, it is by human ingenuity that knowledge is accumulated on how to develop goods and services. Human ingenuity determines from the simplest to the most complex products and services, the plant and equipment and technologies that could be designed and built for the purpose. Furthermore, human ingenuity is responsible for identifying and securing the kinds of goods and services we wish to use.

The other dimension views human resources development as the ultimate end of development, which is developing people from both a material and non-material point of view. We are not merely concerned with the production of goods and services for their own sake. One is ultimately concerned with the utilization of the fruits of increased production for improving the human condition: giving people the possibility of being better fed, better educated and healthier, thus allowing them to enjoy lives of dignity and self-respect.

I wish to first expand on the concept of human resources as a means to development. Knowledge is a principal means through which human beings contribute to the production of goods and services. This involves the application of technology and is therefore linked to a country's capacity to generate, acquire, adapt and utilize technology.

The Knowledge Revolution

In the world today, a virtual knowledge revolution is taking place with the emergence of new technologies in many fields, examples being biotechnology, information technology and the materials sciences. I shall comment briefly on biotechnology and information technology due to their special relevance to development prospects in Jamaica and the Caribbean.

"Biotechnology" is a new term for something old – the study of how life works and how living things and their products can be applied for man's purposes. Examples are the fermentation of beer and rum, pharmaceutical manufacturing, new cloning plant techniques and new chemical manufacturing. In recent years, great excitement has been occasioned by the dramatic advances in genetic engineering in agriculture and other fields. The advantages of genetic engineering are apparent in the production of disease-resistant plants and animals and the enabling of higher yields of crops that have greater uniformity in size and appearance. The advantages are already becoming apparent in livestock, fruit and vegetable production.

At the same time, new advances in technology are leading to the development of artificial products to replace natural products. Two examples of importance to the Caribbean are the production of artificial sweeteners as substitutes for natural sugar and the laboratory production of cocoa butter as a replacement for the natural product.

As with older types of technology, the new technologies are associated with both positive and negative effects. It is incumbent upon us to achieve mastery over this technology to harness the benefits and minimize the negative effects.

The University of the West Indies (UWI) is already engaged in research and training at all three of its campuses. At the Mona Campus, the recently opened Biotechnology Centre is of paramount importance for postgraduate training and research. Significant work has begun in tissue culture and other areas. The Biotechnology Centre is working on projects in collaboration with government and private industry on the propagation of many crops, not limited to Irish potatoes, ginger, cassava, bananas, plantains, yams and sweet potatoes.

Information technology is concerned with the collection, processing and transmission of information. It is the outgrowth of the development in computer technology and related artificial intelligence systems.

Without denying the importance of the human mind to development we should acknowledge that computers have become almost indispensable to human existence. Today, computers enable transport reservation and accommodation systems. Computers also link continental inventory systems, accelerate financial transactions, manage complex systems, run traffic lights and bus systems, control electricity production and transmission and keep government records. The brains of robots control automated factories and operate remote sensing and communications satellites.[1]

The radical transformation brought about by computer technology in production has spread to virtually every sector of the economy. It not only affects the manufacture of highly capital-intensive plants and equipment but has also spread to labour-intensive goods such as textiles. For instance, in the Federal Republic of Germany, over 60 percent of textile production is computerized.

In the field of intelligence systems, it is reported that Japan hopes to bring a fully robotized automobile plant into commercial production by 1993. Japan has also been the leader in introducing computerized "just in time" production systems which have significantly reduced the need to hold inventories of raw materials and components. For example, it is reported that United States firms average nine months of inventory stock, while Japanese firms are able to manage with less than two months' stock.[2]

Knowledge and World Trade

Knowledge-based products have become one of the fastest-growing categories in international trade. Exports of high technology products accounted for 21 percent of the Organization for Economic Cooperation and Development (OECD) exports of manufactured goods in 1985, as against 16 percent ten years earlier. The growth of trade in high technology products has been associated with the phenomenal growth in Japanese exports, allowing Japan to be in the enviable position of being one of the three largest exporting countries in the world, the United States and Germany being the other two in that group. Japanese exports of high technology products alone increased from just under 12 percent of its total exports in 1975 to nearly 20 percent in 1985.

The expansion of high technology trade, particularly in engineering products, has also been associated with the emergence of the "South-East Asian Four" (Hong Kong, the Republic of Korea, Singapore and Taiwan) as major exporters, with their combined share in world exports (8 percent), being greater than that of the individual shares of Britain and France. There can be little doubt that the changes being brought about by knowledge in international trade are leading to far-reaching shifts in the structure of world production and trade, shifts that will have profound implications for the distribution of economic power among countries, with concomitant consequences for international economic relations.

Computerization may have even more profound implications for Jamaica and the Caribbean regarding production and the external trade of services. I shall return to that subject in the next section. But the brief illustrations that I have given on the character of the knowledge revolution in the two fields to which I have referred already pose many important issues for our community.

Research and Development

Growth in the knowledge base of a country springs from its efforts in the field of research, education and training and the relevance of these efforts to production possibilities. I shall return later to education and training, but one can ask here: how adequate is the research effort to development needs, and how supportive is the environment to the intensification of research activity?

This is not the occasion to engage in a detailed overview of research efforts. Such descriptions can be found in the reports of the UWI on its work, which are available from the university campuses and from the reports of agencies such as the Scientific Research Council. The information shows that for a small country and region, Jamaica and the English-speaking Caribbean have not done badly in their research effort in comparison with neighbouring Latin American countries.

For example, I commend to you the *Report of the Inter-American Bank on Economic and Social Progress*, 1988, which contains a comparative analysis of research performance in the fields of science and technology. The report shows that Jamaica and Trinidad and Tobago were among the ten countries in Latin America with the largest number of scientific papers published.

Where the English-speaking Caribbean is less successful is in the commercialization of research results. The research should be used to produce new goods and services and upgrade the production of existing ones. Yet, the commercialization of research is only made possible through a nation's expenditure on research and development.

The data show that developed countries tend to spend about 1 to 3 percent of their gross national product (GNP) on research and development. For Jamaica, a rough estimate is that about 1/8 of 1 percent is being expended on research and development.[3] It is doubtful whether any of the CARICOM countries have registered a better performance.

Many commentators have already emphasized that if we are to make the transition to the new scientific age, a significantly stepped-up effort in research and development is an urgent and imperative need. On the university's part, we are deliberating upon strengthening postgraduate studies and research.

Among other things, we are hoping to establish, in collaboration with the private sector, science and enterprise parks, which would provide a range of research and development and management services to the private sector, especially to businesses in the start-up stage. In the next section, I shall return to the computer revolution and the question of production and trade in services.

The Production and Export of Services

I have already referred to the impact of the computer revolution on production and trade in services. This has led to a fundamental re-thinking of the role of the services sector in economic growth and development.

In the early literature on the subject, services were thought to be of secondary importance to an economy. One school of thought held that services only assumed importance in an economy when it had reached a postindustrial stage, where societies could afford the luxury of allocating an increasing proportion of their resources to service activities such as personal services and leisure. This perspective did not accord with the reality in many developing countries, where the services sector sometimes accounted for the largest proportion of production and employment. Accordingly, another hypothesis was developed, which viewed services as the residual or informal sector in the economy that accommodated people who could not get wage employment in the higher productivity formal sectors. Services were therefore defined as the low productivity sector *par excellence*, characterized by activities such as household service and petty trading.

The application of computer technology to the services sector has now prompted a re-examination of its role and importance. There was a new recognition in many developed countries that services had become a major source of growth over the 1980s, characterized by high-value products and high-paying jobs. Services have also become important in international trade, accounting currently for about one-fifth of the value of world trade in goods. Services fall into two broad categories. The first category includes producer services, which constitute inputs into the production process, for example, transport, telecommunications, design, marketing and finance. The second category includes consumer services: that is, services that are directly consumed, for example, travel, tourism and hairdressing. There are borderline cases such as health and educational services where controversy continues about the category in which they should be placed.

It is now thought that a country's competitive edge in the production of goods is significantly affected by the importance of producer services in the economy and their competitiveness. Up-to-date statistics on producer services are not available. However, in 1981 producer services represented 14 percent of the value of manufacturing output in the Federal Republic of Germany, 16 percent in Italy and 22 percent in France. Other information confirms the growing importance of producer services such as business support services and telecommunications in determining the competitive position of countries.

Japan is a particularly interesting case. Since the early 1970s, the rapid growth of the services sector has been led by the expansion of producer services. From 1972 to 1986 the number of newly established firms increased by 120 percent for producer services, while for consumer and public services the increases were 22 percent and 27 percent, respectively. Likewise, the number of employees in producer services increased by 112 percent, while the corresponding increases for consumer and public services were 30 percent and 60 percent, respectively.[4]

Services have also become a major element in international trade as computerization has made tradable a number of services, which have hitherto been confined to national boundaries. Among the rapidly growing new services in international trade are cleaning services, courier services, security services and credit card verification. Computerization has also been partly responsible for the explosive growth in international financial and securities trading. It is estimated that approximately US$60 trillion of transactions take place in the world's major financial markets every day. The value of international financial transactions has become a substantial multiple of the value of merchandise trade. Today, trade tends to follow finance, whereas traditionally it had been the other way around.

Services in Developing Countries

Developing countries are beginning to attach importance to the services trade. Four developing countries, namely Singapore, Mexico, Saudi Arabia and Egypt, are among the top twenty exporters of services in the world's economy.

A major study commissioned by the Government of Singapore recommended that the promotion of services should be given high priority in government policy, placing equal emphasis on manufacturing and services and making these two sectors the twin engines for Singapore's future growth. Attention is being given to strengthening the international competitive position of various sophisticated services in which Singapore has built up expertise, for example, in air and seaport management, engineering, consultancy and business services.

Mexico has traditionally relied on services such as tourism, processing services and re-insurance to provide the bulk of its foreign exchange earnings from services. However, Mexico has recently been improving its competitive position in non-traditional areas such as architecture and construction engineering and is currently giving attention to the diversification of the services sector in the context of industrial restructuring. Saudi Arabia is selling services connected with the petroleum industry, whereas Egypt is relying upon a mix of tourism, engineering and construction, and labour services.

Several other developing countries are attempting to develop a competitive edge in some of the newer services. India is becoming a significant exporter of computer software, raising its exports of software from US$22 million in 1984 to US$103 million in 1988. Tunisia is concentrating on exporting software to Arabic countries. Bahrain is establishing an international trade centre to become a regional centre for merchandizing in the Middle East. Colombia is trying to develop the export of health services, whereas the Dominican Republic is endeavouring to grow its economy by establishing free zones for services exports.

Although India is a heavily populated country and is for that reason a special case, it is nonetheless a good example of how scientific and technological capability, including computer expertise, can lay the base for thriving service industries. India has approximately two and a half million scientific and technical personnel educated at the tertiary level and several million more high school science graduates. It possesses the world's third-largest pool of scientific and technical skills after the United States and the Soviet Union. Its software firms are targeting the United States market where fluency in English gives them a competitive edge. They are also doing well in Europe, where the industry is handicapped by manpower shortages. For instance, it is reported that about four hundred electronic data specialists are required in the Federal Republic of Germany. This provides an opening for developing countries such as India, with its skilled and relatively inexpensive manpower. However, the recruitment of highly trained specialists by developed countries, known as "body shopping", is creating concern that India will be denuded of its specialist manpower. Joint venturing between local and overseas firms in areas such as software development is seen as one way of stemming the outflow of trained people.

Initiatives for Developing the Services Sector

If Jamaica and the rest of the Caribbean are to make any significant progress with the development of the new computer-based services, a number of actions will need to be taken.

First, it will be necessary for a significant part of the labour force, particularly young persons with secondary and tertiary level education, to acquire computer literacy. This effort will have to start at UWI and in other tertiary institutions and schools, and will also need to involve on-the-job training. In this vein, computer literacy education and training will become the norm.

Second, at the university level, efforts will have to be intensified to expand and upgrade programmes in computer science to produce more software engineers. UWI will need to undertake vigorous recruitment of computer scientists and establish more competitive levels of remuneration for them. It is noteworthy that at the present time, several faculty vacancies at the senior level are unfilled because of low salaries. The university will also be obliged to encourage more research and development work in software programmes.

Third, the governments should adopt definite policies regarding the importation of hardware and consider whether imports of computer hardware should be permitted on a duty-free basis.

Fourth, an adequate supply of technicians who can service and maintain the equipment must be trained. Hardware is normally purchased on a package basis, which includes the training of technicians. Governments should encourage competition among suppliers so that the best terms for equipment/training packages are secured.

The points above assume that computerization will form part of an overall strategy for the development of the services sector. This strategy should involve the targeting of specific service activities and the development of locations to achieve economies of scale. The strategy should also involve aggressive efforts to assist local companies to find joint venture partners which will give them access to specific niches in export markets.

As already mentioned, the idea of free zones for services, which parallel free zones for goods, is beginning to gain ground and could be considered by governments and businesses in the region.

Turning to the specific service activities that deserve consideration, a few preliminary and general comments can be made. In the field of producer services, most governments already recognize the need to improve the physical and economic infrastructure to support the growth of production for the local market and for export. Attention is now being given to upgrading internal and external transport services, which are generally thought to be deficient in both quantity and quality.

A similar situation prevails with telephone and external communications services. Several governments are implementing, or are in the process of formulating, plans for improvement in those services. The return of Cable and Wireless Limited to Jamaica and the intensification of activities in the territories indicate service improvement. Other companies are also involved in the supply of state-of-the-art equipment and training.

Banking, insurance and securities trading are growing rapidly and reaching a stage of sophistication that should permit them to go beyond the domestic market. Governments have expressed interest in the development of a CARICOM Stock Exchange, starting first with the listing of securities on existing exchanges in Barbados, Jamaica, and Trinidad and Tobago. However, given the close interaction which is now developing between securities and other financial markets, partly reflected in the financial conglomerating which is taking place, CARICOM countries may well have to consider establishing a Caribbean Common Market in financial services. This should serve as a learning phase for the development of extra-regional exports of those services.

Some countries are also building capabilities in other producer services, which could provide an initial base for eventual export development. These services include engineering, management consultancy, accounting and auditing services, and market research and advertising services. The growth of informal commercial importers in wholesale and retail trade raises the question whether this potential should in fact be harnessed for developing Jamaica as an international merchandizing centre. Jamaica would identify sources of quality goods in high demand and supply them competitively to neighbouring countries.

Regarding consumer services, the expansion and diversification of the tourist industry is a top priority. But with this could come expansion in a number of other related services such as entertainment, education and health. I have mentioned before that the world market for cultural tourism seems to be growing with the development of tourist packages that include instruction in the culture of the destination and, in some instances, language training. Similarly, Jamaica is among the countries that are beginning to cater to the diet consciousness of their customers. Health care packages are becoming important in the industry. Countries that are able to offer quality health care inexpensively could develop a significant competitive edge in the trade.

In my address to the first Conference of Caribbean Economists in July 1987, I made the more general point that some countries in the region have over different periods of time been exporters of educational and medical services. The prospects of developing such exports on a larger scale deserve investigation.

This section ends with this thought. If we are to take the fullest advantage of the opportunities for developing the services sector, bold and innovative approaches will have to be adopted at all levels to upgrade and develop the educational system.

Education and Training as Avenues for Economic Growth

The state of knowledge in a country is ultimately linked to the development of its educational system. It is clear from what has been said about the knowledge revolution that the educational system has a central role to play in developing a country's potential. Some evidence is available that suggests that sequentially later industrializations have been characterized by higher levels of mass education. The second industrial revolution in the United States and Germany involved more educated populations than the first industrial revolution in Britain, and there are indications that at least Japan and Korea began their industrializations with more educated populations than those of Britain, Germany or the United States in earlier periods.[5]

In 1903, there were five students in British universities for every ten thousand in the population. In 1985 the comparable figure for Korea was 217.5 students. Indeed, both Japan and South Korea have been maintaining particularly high enrolments at the secondary and tertiary levels. In 1986, Japan had 96 percent of its secondary age population enrolled in secondary schools, and 29 percent of its tertiary age cohort enrolled in tertiary institutions. In the Republic of Korea, 95 percent and 33 percent were comparable ratios.

Deficiencies in Education

Turning to our own situation, complaints about the educational system in Jamaica and in several other Caribbean countries are now legion. Chronic shortage of qualified teachers, deteriorating buildings and equipment and shortage of materials are among the most pervasive problems. The poor quality of the educational system is an outcome of the 1970s and 1980s. Prior to that, Jamaica and the rest of the region had a reputation for good education. Many persons who have occupied important positions in the post-war period had only a primary school education. During the colonial period and in the pre-independence years, Jamaica and Barbados, in particular, supplied teachers to English-speaking countries in West Africa. At the secondary level, some countries in the region exported educational services, taking students from nearby Latin American countries who desired a secondary education in English. Some of these students were the children of West Indian migrants who had a deep respect for the high standard of schooling in the region.

Although standards were high, relatively few persons were being educated. In 1950, the gross enrolment ratio in primary education and secondary education in Jamaica was 68 percent and 15 percent, respectively. This compares with current figures of around 100 percent at the primary level and over 50 percent at the secondary level. The rapid expansion in enrolments started in the 1970s when the Government of Jamaica adopted the policy of free secondary education. However, during the 1980s, the effective implementation of this policy was constrained by decreasing public expenditure on education, which had the effect of reducing standards. Valued in constant 1974 dollars, the recurrent expenditure on education fell from a peak of $129 million in 1977–78 to a low of $93 million in 1984–85. Reports indicate that the recurrent expenditure on education reached an even further low in 1987–88.

The principal problem in primary and secondary education has become one of quality rather than quantity.[6] The tertiary system also has serious deficiencies in quantity, and in some cases in quality. At the quantitative level, the gross enrolment ratio in Jamaica is no more than 6 percent or about one-third of the average for middle-income developing countries.

The disparity is particularly marked in science and technology. I often cite the case of Singapore – admittedly a special one – with a population not dissimilar to Jamaica (2.6 million as against 2.4) but with about ten times the number of students enrolled at the tertiary level in science and technology. Also, compare the regional picture in relation to engineering. The so-called newly industrialized countries have a range of 20 percent to 40 percent of their post-secondary students enrolled in engineering. The largest segment of engineering students in the CARICOM area is at UWI, where there are eight hundred engineering students of a total enrolment in all faculties of almost twelve thousand.

In the natural sciences, the ten-year period 1977–78 to 1987–88 saw virtually no growth in the number of students registered for a first degree at the Mona Campus. The numbers remained almost static at just over one thousand although there was a small increase in the number of postgraduate students.

There has been virtually no growth in the intake of students into the natural sciences at UWI because of the inadequate preparation at the secondary level in mathematics and science. The inadequate preparation is also manifested in the high failure rate in preliminary and introductory courses in subjects such as mathematics and computer sciences. In 1987–88, the failure rate for the preliminary course and the introductory course in mathematics was 37 percent and 40 percent, respectively. In computer science, the failure rate in the introductory course was 35 percent.

I have been drawing illustrations from university education to discuss deficiencies in the tertiary system, but one should not confuse the terms "university education" and "tertiary education". The University is only one part of the tertiary system. Tertiary education refers to the entire range of post-secondary education, including the College of Arts, Science and Technology (CAST), technical and vocational colleges, community colleges, teacher training colleges, agricultural training institutions and the work/study schemes that usually involve formal apprenticeships.

Some commentaries on the deficiencies in tertiary education in science and technology have missed this distinction and have argued erroneously that the training of technicians is of higher priority than the training of scientists. The training needs of the two categories are complementary rather than competitive. Scientists and engineers require technicians to do their work; the reverse also applies.

Overseas Students

One of the manifestations of deficiencies in the educational system is the large number of students studying abroad. According to UNESCO data, in the period 1983–85, CARICOM countries had over eight thousand students studying abroad, of which Jamaica contributed over two thousand. These figures may well be underestimated, since a proportion of people going abroad as visitors or migrants also tend to take advantage of educational opportunities. It would not be unsurprising if it were discovered that CARICOM countries are spending US$20 million per annum on foreign study, which would be a sufficient sum of money to sustain a fourth campus at the UWI. Moreover, the potential brain drain involved is significant. It is desirable to send a proportion of our students abroad. Nonetheless, a detailed study of the present situation might show that a significant number of these students could be attracted towards local study if the tertiary educational system were strengthened.

Two factors favouring an overseas education are the greater flexibility that exists in admission requirements and the wider choice of courses and specializations available to students.

At UWI, significant progress has been made in recent years in making admissions requirements flexible. Thus, it is now possible to secure entry at the University of Cambridge and University of London Ordinary ("O") levels into degree programmes in natural sciences and in arts programmes offered in the evenings. It is also possible to secure partial or full accreditation for a number of diploma and certificate programmes offered by other tertiary institutions, thereby reducing the time students are required to spend on campus in completing a degree. Students at the Sir Arthur Lewis Community College in St. Lucia and the Antigua State College can now do the first year of their degree in arts, sciences and social sciences. This opportunity will be extended to other tertiary level institutions as circumstances permit. The Bachelor of Education degree is now being offered to students through special arrangements with the Mico Teacher Training College in Jamaica and the College of The Bahamas.

The proposed introduction of a semester-type system by UWI starting on a phased basis in the academic year of 1990/1991 will give further flexibility to the process of accreditation and also open possibilities for introducing a wider choice of courses.

Training

Serious deficiencies also exist in the area of training. There are only a few opportunities for obtaining a technical or industrial skill. Accordingly, one finds that out of the 203,000 persons that were unemployed in Jamaica in 1988, 89 percent of them had received no training. There is also limited enrolment in technical and vocational schools. Ministry of Education statistics for 1986–87 reveal that only 8,611 students or 3.6 percent of total secondary school enrolments were in technical high schools and in vocational and agricultural schools. Furthermore, these schools suffer from shortage of equipment, space and trained teachers, as do others in the system.

A factor favouring late industrializers like Jamaica is the reduction in the time required to acquire an industrial skill. At the start of the first industrial revolution, a typical apprenticeship lasted five to seven years. Today, modern technology has simplified industrial skills to such a degree that vocational training centres in developed countries are able to graduate technicians in a fraction of that time.

Resources for Education and Training

The central issue facing the upgrading and enlargement of the educational system in Jamaica, and to some extent in other Caribbean countries, is finding the necessary resources. There is little room available to governments for increasing expenditure on education. In the typical case, the government is already devoting 5 percent to 6 percent of GNP to expenditure on education, which compares well with developed countries and other developing countries at similar levels of development. It can be argued that Jamaica can modestly increase the percentage of its national budget devoted to education from the present level of 13 percent and bring it close to the average for middle income developing countries, which is between 15 and 16 percent. But this may not involve any absolute increase in expenditure since the government is expected to sharply reduce the overall public expenditure in order to cut its budget deficit from its present high level of 9 percent of GNP. Prospects for revenue growth are also at best modest since it is unlikely that the economy itself will achieve anything but small increments of growth in the short term.

Given these set of circumstances, the potential for improving the educational system will depend on several factors. These include the achievement of greater cost-effectiveness in education so that greater value is received for money spent; the ability of the government to re-allocate expenditure from tertiary and secondary education to primary education; and the readiness and ability of private sources to make up for the shortfall at those two levels.

In other words, we have reached a situation in Jamaica and in most of the English-speaking Caribbean where free education at the secondary and tertiary levels is no longer feasible. If we are to continue to have free education at these levels, we will have to accept the deterioration of standards. The demands of economic development under present conditions continue to make free higher education an unrealistic choice.

Economic development is about choices. Parents, especially those with incomes, have to decide the importance to assign to education in their household expenditure based on their income levels. They will decide the priority to give education vis a vis other investments, such as motor cars, satellite dishes, and other state-of-the-art appliances and equipment. Parents and their children who are direct beneficiaries of these levels of education should assume full or partial responsibility for the cost of their education. Modalities will have to be found for expanding student loan schemes, with varying levels of concessionality depending on the household income of the student involved.

An approach to the financing of education along these lines combines the principles of equity and the ability to pay. Providing for the full public financing of an improved system of primary education ensures that all students, irrespective of their parents' income, will receive a sound educational foundation. At the same time, households would be required to contribute to the cost of higher levels of education on terms that take into account their ability to pay. Financing is not the only area in the educational system that requires reform, but financing can open the way for other improvements, such as the maintenance of the physical plant and the retention of quality teachers.

One should also not overstate the relationship between education and economic growth. There are no spontaneous forces that will work automatically to transform an educated labour force into new economic activity. Countries – South Korea being an example – have undergone periods of unemployment of their educated population. Nonetheless, the existence of an educated labour force provides a starting point for economic growth if entrepreneurs come forward to utilize the existing endowment of skills. This leads to the question of entrepreneurship, which I shall discuss in the following section.

A Culture of Production

In the study of the development process, much attention has been given to the role of the entrepreneur in economic development. International studies on the economic impact of entrepreneurship have mostly been unable to identify the precise contribution made by entrepreneurship. In his classical study of the issue, Joseph Schumpeter depicted the entrepreneur as the catalyst, taking the lead in risk-taking and innovation. This perception continues to dominate up to the present day and accurately describes the role played by many of the successful businessmen of our time, especially in North America and Europe.

In the case of the late industrialized nations such as Japan, the Republic of Korea, Singapore and Taiwan, it is still debatable how much of their success is attributable to individual effort, as against concerted efforts in strategic planning by the private and the public sectors. The direct role of the state has been even more pronounced in countries such as Brazil, India and Mexico.

In general, the evidence suggests that a key feature of the industrialization process is the maintenance of a supportive environment for increasing production. Government is crucial in this effort, not so much as the producers but as the providers of production incentives. These incentives cover many areas. Examples are encouraging innovation, research and development, maintaining appropriate macro-economic policies, implementing measures that directly impact the plant level and influencing both management and labour to achieve and sustain high productivity and cost-effectiveness. However, the encouragement of production is not a matter for the government alone. It has to be a broadly based effort by society to adopt a greater orientation towards production.

Production Culture

A production culture is an ethic favouring increased production and competitiveness. A production culture characterizes most of the growth and development success stories in the world. This type of success has manifested itself in high rates of corporate and personal savings, a highly motivated management and labour force continuously aspiring to improve work performance, and a strong national commitment to performance through hard work, discipline and respect for achievement. Although in some cases, these elements are believed to have sprung from traditional cultures, they are essentially man-made. Nothing inhibits a country from developing a culture of production if its leadership is inspiring the population to do so at national, community and enterprise levels. In Jamaica and the Caribbean, greater attention needs to be paid to the several elements that constitute a culture of production. One is the greater recognition of achievement. I quote here some frequently quoted statements by Sir Arthur Lewis on the mindset needed if Caribbean people are to succeed.

You must be willing to work hard, while the rest of your companions are at play. You must be willing to practice over and over again, until you get it right. You must be highly self-critical. You must be humble enough to welcome, analyze and apply the criticisms of others, or you will never learn. There is no doubt that achievers have a special type of personality. This drive for achievement is not identical with brainpower. Many people with excellent brains achieve nothing, while men with moderate brains can be highly successful if they have the drive to achieve.

An achiever feels an acute sense of failure every time he has to make an excuse for non-performance, however valid. But in some Third World countries, one gets the impression that the largest industry is the manufacture of excuses for non-performance, and pride in the artistry of one's excuses is widespread.

> We shall not be well endowed with business types until our society learns to appreciate the business-like personality and absorbs this appreciation into the cultural framework of boyhood, girlhood and adolescence.[7]

An area that cries out for improvement is the work habit. Complaints about the tolerance of lateness, absenteeism, long breaks during working hours and slacking on the job are frequent. Insufficient respect is paid to deadlines and the completion of jobs and contracts on time tends to be the exception rather than the rule. This attitude affects productivity and competitiveness and is particularly harmful to sectors and industries engaged in international trade where the reliability of supply and rigorous adherence to delivery dates are absolutely indispensable for success.

Many of these weaknesses reflect a failure of supervision and inadequate delegation of responsibility. Training can play a role here to sensitize managers and supervisors to the appropriate delegation of responsibility and to undertake effective monitoring of the performance of colleagues under their direct responsibility. Management should try to work out with unions the incentives and penalties that could help to reduce and eliminate these weaknesses.

More deep-seated are the attitudes of complaining, lamenting the weaknesses in the local situation and extolling the virtues to be found in countries overseas. We have to be sensitive to local deficiencies and act to correct them, not merely to play the role of armchair critics. We should develop the confidence to believe that we are able to tackle our own problems, thereby contributing to the onward march towards progress.

At a more general level, the people of the region, especially the young, need to be exposed to role models of success in business and other economic activities. This poses a challenge to educational institutions and the media to develop and present local cases of achievement and success for the enlightenment of the population.

A questionable practice is the tendency to restrict outside competition in employment by permitting outsiders to take up employment only where there are no nationals available to do the particular job. The work permit legislation which regulates the employment of foreigners had initial justification when employers tended to give preference to foreigners, even when there were local citizens of equivalent or superior qualifications.

However, reports indicate that some CARICOM countries have refused to grant work permits to nationals from other CARICOM countries when nationals did not have the basic qualifications for the job or had patently lower qualifications.

If CARICOM countries are to progress with export development and new activities such as services, the allotment of work permits needs to be reassessed. This will ensure that the region's professional and skilled people are able to compete against the best available talent from outside. The indulgence of mediocrity, not to speak of incompetence, is a recipe for economic failure, however congenial it might be on nationalist grounds.

At the same time, Jamaica and other CARICOM countries should give greater incentives for and recognition to hard work and achievement. Although productivity incentives have been introduced by many companies, they are still not a standard feature of salary and wage agreements. Salary and wage structures in the public sector make little or no provision for rewarding high performances. Overall, insufficient recognition is given at the national level to the successes achieved by scientists and other professionals in their respective occupations.

Self-employment and the development of small businesses should receive more incentives and greater support. These could take the form of so-called incubator services, which help the start-up businessperson to transform an idea into a bankable project. Retraining schemes could have a similar effect by assisting people to change their occupations and careers, especially when they wish to enter fields of high growth potential.

Policymakers should take care to ensure that such services are properly distributed between urban and rural areas so that sectors such as agriculture and agribusiness receive the support required. The extent that new employment opportunities are created in the rural areas may lead to less migration to towns. Internal migration to the principal urban areas in Jamaica has been growing at about 7 percent per annum, which creates pressure on jobs, housing and social services in the towns while leaving capacity under-utilized in the countryside.

I must mention the macro-economic policy framework, which has received considerable attention recently in the context of adjustment programmes. The private sector has generally welcomed the deregulation of economic activity in so far as it involved the abolition of cumbersome and time-consuming administrative controls and procedures. However, concern has been expressed about the reduction or removal of protection for local industries. This may have some justification where the need for infant industry protection can be substantiated, bearing in mind that foreign producers are often protected by their own governments.

Caribbean governments need to carefully consider the circumstances in which unilateral trade liberalization is in the national interest. Where continuing protection is justified, they need to tighten their surveillance machinery to ensure that the industries concerned do not receive excess protection and that protection is phased out once they begin to stand on their feet.

In general, in an economy like Jamaica which relies heavily on foreign trade, at least two factors should be taken into consideration. Macro-economic policy, especially monetary policy, which deals with the availability and terms of credit, and fiscal policy, which deals with taxes and government expenditure, should be policy-neutral, in the sense that they do not favour one sector over another. In particular, they should not favour protection for the domestic market as against protection for export.

While this is unquestioned as a principle, it should not be applied simplistically. In the real world, one has to take a strategic view of the economy and decide which sectors and activities need special encouragement due to their importance to the growth and competitiveness of the economy in the long term. For example, import substitution should be encouraged to build an export capability over time.

In general, a comprehensive and well-formulated policy framework for improving the environment for investment and production is now a matter of top priority, which governments already recognize. Governments also recognize the necessity to involve the private sector in the formulation and implementation of such a framework. This includes the question of macro-economic policy, notwithstanding the fact that countries like Jamaica, which are implementing International Monetary Fund (IMF) stabilization adjustment programmes, have little room in which to manoeuvre.

Human Development as the Purpose of Economic Development

In this final section, I would like to turn to the second dimension of human resources development. This concerns developing the capability of people to lead fulfilling lives and gives expression to the idea that economic development does not only involve increasing the production of goods and services but is ultimately concerned with improving the human condition.

The Trickle-Down of Growth

The early literature on economic development presented the view that economic growth would trickle down to the broad masses of the population through increased employment and also through the utilization of increases in government revenue to improve social services such as education, health and social security.

The experiences of many countries during the 1960s cast doubt upon the effectiveness of trickle-down mechanisms, especially in relation to employment. In several countries, increases in employment tended to lag behind the growth in output. Evidence began to accumulate that the lower-income groups in the population – the so-called bottom 40 percent – were not experiencing improvements in their life conditions commensurate with the overall expansion which had taken place in the economy.

Basic Needs

This led to the widespread shift towards basic needs strategies of development which attempted to directly target the basic needs of the masses of the population for items such as food, shelter, clothing, education and health. Although these strategies had a strong rationale and wide appeal, they ran into trouble in several countries. There were instances where governments attempted to implement particularly ambitious targets over too short a period of time, often employing draconian measures to change patterns of demand and supply.

Many of these measures did not work and created severe tensions and economic imbalances. Another feature was the expansion of the state sector, which critics alleged crowded out private investment and promoted governmental inefficiency, political patronage and corruption. Far from building capabilities, the attempt to expand the provision of some services too rapidly failed to achieve its objective. For example, too rapid an expansion in education and health had led to deteriorating standards. It was generally perceived that basic needs strategies were the product of romantic notions of self-reliance, which encouraged the adoption of autocratic policies even in very small countries with a high structural dependency upon foreign trade.

Market-oriented Strategies

During the 1980s, a large number of developing countries shifted towards more market-oriented strategies for economic growth. This invariably involved the deregulation of the economy through the privatization of state enterprises, the abolition of price controls and subsidies and the adoption of foreign trade liberalization. These elements were thought indispensable to the achievement of growth competitiveness as the economy sought to move towards a path of export-oriented development. This strategy also required flexible exchange rates and a positive real rate of interest that reflected the true scarcity of capital. Furthermore, fiscal discipline was a central element in the form of a sharp reduction in public sector deficits, which had hitherto crowded out private investment and were an instrumental and major source of inflationary pressure.

The pressure of exports was most evident on heavily indebted countries which as a matter of urgency needed to generate additional foreign exchange to service their debt. The policy mix described above came to constitute the core of IMF/World Bank stabilization and adjustment programmes with indebted countries.

Without entering the controversy about whether these policies have succeeded or are likely to succeed, we can see that it was clear from an early stage that they were having a disproportionately negative impact on the poorer and the more vulnerable groups in society. This caused deep concern in several parts of the international community, which in turn led to the introduction of programmes to alleviate the negative social impact of adjustment.

These programmes, first started in Ghana in 1986, typically include infant feeding programmes, food for work projects, start-up finance for redundant workers to engage in self-employment, and community-based care and education projects. Social impact programmes can help to alleviate the worst cases of distress, but they are no panacea. Essentially they are designed to allow the economy to buy time until the process of adjustment takes hold and sustained economic growth returns. A fundamental reason why problems of social impact arise is that structural rigidities in the economy impede the movement of labour and other factors of production from sectors that are contracting to those capable of expansion. Therefore, the diversification of production and markets is at the heart of the adjustment process since they make the economy more adaptable to changes taking place both at home and abroad.

Supply-centred Adjustment

It is evident that countries that implement a stabilization/adjustment programme follow a two-track approach. They push for a restoration of economic growth through the diversification of production and markets while simultaneously ensuring that the most vulnerable groups in the society are protected from drastic declines in their living standards. Such an approach will require somewhat different stabilization/ adjustment packages than we have seen so far. The promotion of diversification entails the targeting of policy measures and finance towards the removal of major supply constraints in the economy, rather than merely giving emphasis to a policy package to contract demand.

Supply-centred adjustment is beginning to gain endorsements from the international community, reflected in the fact that the World Bank is now taking a leading role in adjustment programmes. However, countries are not yet receiving sufficient resources from the multilateral institutions to implement effective supply-centred programmes. In several cases, there is still a negative net transfer of resources to the multilateral institutions, despite the programmes that have been implemented. The expectation that private lending and direct investment will resume on a scale sufficient to bring about a positive net transfer of resources is proving to be increasingly less realistic.

The Dilemma of Growth versus Distribution

One should observe in parenthesis that the basic issue underlying the discussion of "trickle down", "basic needs" and "social impact" is the age-old dilemma of growth versus distribution. This dilemma continues to be one of the most elusive questions in economics. It should occasion no surprise to discover that it remains a highly controversial issue with sharply divided positions and that a country's experiences with the problem vary over both time and space. What this boils down to is the need for each country to formulate its economic policy not on the supposition of universally held truths but on the basis of its concrete realities, including the political space that policymakers perceive themselves to have.

Relevance to the Contemporary Situation in Jamaica

How does all of this apply to the contemporary situation in Jamaica, where an adjustment effort has been under way since the latter part of the 1970s? A case study of Jamaica's experience has been included in the latest issue of the United Nations World Economy Survey. As far as the social impact is concerned, the study shows that despite the efforts that were made to provide a safety net for household consumption, most of the social indicators moved negatively.

According to UNICEF, between 1978 and 1985, the incidence of mild malnutrition rose from 8 percent to 39 percent and the prevalence of stunted growth in infants from 6 percent to 14 percent. In that period, real expenditure on health per head of population fell from J$78 to J$54, or by 30 percent. Another source has estimated that in constant 1980/81 values, real expenditure on education in Jamaica fell from its peak of J$333M in 1976–77 to reach a low of J$193M in 1985–86.[8] Furthermore, the migration of Jamaicans to the United States has continued in the 1980s at roughly twenty thousand per year or nearly twice the level of the 1970s.

The United Nations study concluded that the basic weakness in the Jamaican economy is the relative absence of structural change. The study makes the point below:

> In sum, the economy today looks similar in fundamental ways to what it was fifteen years ago. It relies on a few export earners, which have few linkages to the rest of the economy, which generate relatively few jobs and which have a high import content.

> Jamaica also has a relatively specialized economy, relying heavily on imports for direct consumption of rich and poor alike. There is a conspicuously unequal distribution of wealth and persistently high unemployment.[9]

How does all of this apply to the contemporary situation in Jamaica? It is widely acknowledged that the task for the future involves maximizing the diversification of production and markets so that the economy becomes more adaptable and more resilient to external shocks and more capable of responding to emerging opportunities. This brings us back to the first issue that I took up, namely the upgrading of human resources as a means towards greater growth and development.

Until we expand the knowledge base and make it more directly supportive of production possibilities, until we become more production-oriented as a people, sustained growth and development may continue to be an empty aspiration. We have a chance during the 1990s to turn the tide and move forward.

This opportunity is made more attractive by the prospect that as we turn to the next century, population growth will begin to decline. According to projections made by Professor G. W. Roberts of UWI, the population of primary school-age children will decline from 550,000 in 1987 to 486,000 in 2007 and of secondary age from 400,000 to 347,000. If we lay good foundations in this decade, our children and our grandchildren will have an improved education, which itself will bring greater material advances and greater self-fulfilment. We cannot afford to fail them.

Notes

1. Forbes, Jeff. 'An Overview of Informatics and Development' from Informatics circa 1987. p. 167.
2. *Business Week*, 6 June 1988. pp. 46–48.
3. Lowe, Henry. *Science and Technology in Jamaica's National Development'* in *Jamaica in Independence*, Rex Nettleford (ed.). Heinemann Publishers (Caribbean) Ltd., 1989.
4. *UNCTAD Trade and Development Report*, 1988. pp. 145–146.
5. Amsden, Alice. *Asia's Next Giant: South Korea and Late Industrialisation*. Oxford University Press, 1989.
6. Miller, Errol. *Educational Development in Independent Jamaica*, Rex Nettleford (ed.). Jamaica in independence.
7. Lewis, Sir Arthur. In the Statement of the President of the Caribbean Development Bank.
8. Boyd, Derick. Personal Communication.
9. United Nations *World Economic Survey*, 1989. p. 184.

Selected Bibliography

Alice Amsden, *Asia's next Giant: South Korea and Late Industrialisation*, Oxford University Press, 1989.
Commonwealth Secretariat, Caribbean Community Secretariat, *Caribbean Development in the Year 2000: Challenges, Prospects and Policies*.
Development Dialogue 1988, 1–2, *The Laws of Life, Another Development and the New Biotechnologies'*.
K. Haq and U. Kirader, 'Development for People.' *North-South Roundtable* 1989.
Inter-American Development Bank, *Economic and Social Progress in Latin America: 1988 and 1989 Reports*.
J. Loubser, R.C. Hughes, Z. Ali, and C. Bourne, *Report on an Institutional Review of the University of the West Indies: 1988*.
Ministry of Education, Jamaica, *Educational Statistics 1986–87.1989*.
OECD, *Information Technology and Economic Prospects*. 1987.
Scientific Research Council, Jamaica, *Final Draft Science and Technology*.
UNESCO, *Statistical Yearbook*, 1987.
United Nations, *Journal of Development Planning* Vol. 19,1989. 'Human Development in the 1980s and Beyond'.
United Nations, *World Economic Survey*, 1989.
UNCTAD, *Trade and Development Report*, 1988.
World Bank, *World Development Report*, 1989. 'Development Indications'.

Chapter 1.2

Issues in Human Resources Development

A Commentary Prepared for the World Bank, 1995
(*Caribbean Dialogue: A Journal of Contemporary Caribbean Policy Issues*, Volume 3, Number 1 (1997))

Introduction

Human resources development is both an end and a means to economic and social development. This essay concentrates on social development, addressing education and training. The essay steps back from the data to identify broad trends, patterns and issues that are in need of greater policy and public attention.

There is widespread recognition in the public and private sectors that more intensive and urgent efforts to upgrade education and training, both in quantitative and qualitative terms, are essential to increase international competitiveness and realize the development potential of countries in the region.

Significant improvements in education and skills attainment are critical to modernizing traditional sectors. These improvements include the development of new lines of production in agriculture and manufacturing and enhancing the services sector. The improvements should be associated with an enlargement of the knowledge base by accelerated and broadly based activities in R&D.

Access

At the present time, the educational and knowledge systems fall notably short of these objectives. Recent data show that the probabilities of educational attainment in the English-speaking Caribbean start with 100 percent at primary level, 55 percent at secondary level, 7 percent at tertiary level other than university and 3 percent at the UWI.

These numbers indicate that the quantitative shortfall is most striking at the tertiary level where gross enrolment ratios are less than one-third of the average for middle-income developing countries, taken as a whole. The tertiary shortfall is particularly marked in science and technology. To cite one example, Jamaica, with a roughly similar population to Singapore, has about one-tenth of Singapore's gross enrolments in science and technology.

The Primary Level

At the primary level, although the gross enrolment ratios compare favourably with other parts of the world, complaints are legion about quality. In virtually every part of the

Caribbean, marked imbalances exist in the availability of places in different schools, also based on urban or rural location. Thus, one finds a situation where heavy overcrowding coexists with significant under-utilization of places. Recent research conducted in Jamaica and Trinidad and Tobago identifies the problem of maldistribution of places in school as requiring immediate attention.

Furthermore, the upkeep of schools is also deficient. Challenges are not limited to dire shortages of textbooks and equipment, the repair of damaged furniture and other facilities and inefficiencies in the day-to-day maintenance of buildings and grounds. A 1994 report of OECS countries showed that of a total of 466 primary schools, 102 were without telephones, 219 without a single typewriter, 202 without libraries and almost 400 without science rooms. Guyana ranks lowest among CARICOM countries in indicators of educational capacity. A survey of infrastructure in 1991 showed that only 10 percent of the schools were in a satisfactory condition. Over half of the students attend schools where no textbooks are available, and more than 70 percent of teachers in several rural and interior areas are untrained.

Perhaps the most serious weaknesses lie in curricula and teaching methods. Efforts have been underway for the better part of three decades to expose students to broad curricula that provide a solid foundation for developing their cognitive and numerical capabilities. Too often, these efforts have not been sustained due to resource constraints. Moreover, teaching methods are out-of-date, emphasizing learning by rote rather than problem-solving. Educators explain that the use of problem-solving methods requires small classes and adequate materials and equipment. These are the exception rather than the rule.

Co-curricular activities are in need of greater attention. A special experiment undertaken in a small sample of Jamaican schools has confirmed the importance of these activities in building leadership, discipline and teamwork. They have proven to be excellent instruments for conflict resolution in schools that hitherto had disturbing levels of violence among students.

One factor affecting school performance is the gender imbalance among teachers, reflected in an extraordinarily high proportion of female to male teachers. It is generally thought that this imbalance contributes in one way or another to low participation, poor academic performance and relatively high drop-out rates among boys in the primary-secondary-tertiary continuum.

The Secondary Level

A critical stage is reached at age eleven when students are streamed. The better performers are registered in the classical secondary schools, essentially of an academic character, while the remainder enters another type of post-primary school, referred to as All-Age, Senior, Comprehensive or Junior Secondary. These latter schools tend to be the most affected in the system, in terms of resources, quantity and quality of staff, as well as programmes.

The programmes in these schools should have a strong practical content, exposing students to "hands-on" activities that would equip and orient them for the world of work. However, due to resource shortages, the usual situation is for the students to be prepared for the same examinations taken by students in the academic stream. Predictably, high rates of failure result particularly in English, Mathematics and Science subjects, illustrated by the pattern of results in the Caribbean Examinations Council (CXC) examinations. In Trinidad and Tobago, one of the best-performing countries in the region, much less than 10 percent of students sitting examinations from Comprehensive/Junior Secondary Schools pass five or more subjects. Moreover, employers complain of hiring students with four to five CXC passes who have difficulties with reading, writing and doing simple computations.

The more academic schools also face difficulties in preparing students in English, Mathematics and Science. Although pass rates are higher in the more academic schools, it is still not unusual to find a less than 50 percent pass rate in some schools. However, this overall profile conceals significant variations between individual countries and individual schools. For instance, Trinidad and Tobago achieves exceptional results in the University of Cambridge Advanced Level examinations, notably in the science subjects. St. Kitts and Nevis is a small island nation, where comparatively high rates of entry into secondary schools and good examination performances are being recorded. It is believed that the relatively favourable performance of secondary schools in Trinidad and Tobago and St. Kitts and Nevis can be attributed to the high quality of teaching, itself a function of the good rates of pay in the school system.

Countries thus have successful examples on which they can draw to correct weaknesses in the secondary system. The inter-country and inter-school sharing of experiences is happening, but not yet on a sufficiently large scale.

Governments, private sectors, non-governmental organizations and external donors have been involved in initiatives to increase the employability of graduates from secondary schools. These have taken the form of supporting teaching in practical subjects, helping to develop computer literacy skills of staff and students and promoting work/study projects. These efforts are all commendable and, though becoming more common, are still on a relatively modest scale due to limited human and financial resources.

Based on rough estimates made by some sources, it is possible that the initial capital requirements for making the entire school population in the English-speaking Caribbean computer literate could exceed US$1 billion. Given that the costs of computer hardware and software are trending downwards, these requirements could be within reach and could be spread over a five- to seven-year period. A genuine national effort will be required to attain this goal.

Apart from equipment and software, a major thrust will be needed in the training and re-training of teachers in educational technology. Teachers' colleges and universities have not made significant progress in implementing educational technology training programmes, partly because of their inability to recruit highly qualified staff due to their uncompetitive salaries. This is a matter to which the local private sector and external donors should give more attention: by contributing towards the cost of faculty development, releasing their own staff on a part-time or secondment basis to assist with teaching, providing overseas technical assistance or topping up local salaries.

A most suitable area for Caribbean nations to cooperate is the tertiary system. Caribbean nations should mobilize the necessary human and financial resources and share expertise in the establishment and management of systems and staff training.

UWI has already indicated its readiness to be the hub of a network of tertiary institutions, tackling issues such as capacity building in educational technology.

Greater and more sustained efforts are also required in the development of apprenticeship schemes. This is a prime area for private sector involvement, and some encouraging developments are taking place. The Youth Training and Employment Partnership Programme (YTEPP) in Trinidad and Tobago, supported by the World Bank, is one example. However, apprenticeship opportunities need to be more fully integrated into the regular operation of all firms and other organizations. So far, they are concentrated among a small number of large companies.

There are complaints about deficiencies in the organization of apprenticeships arising from inadequate supervision and evaluation of apprentices. These point to weaknesses that need to be corrected by human resources development specialists in firms. Of note, UWI's Institute of Business has begun to provide HRD training for the private sector.

The Reform of the Primary and Secondary Systems

At both the national and sub-regional levels, governments are working on the reform of the primary and secondary systems. It seems likely that in several countries, the eleven-plus examinations, the examinations taken by eleven-year-olds, will be eliminated. The examinations will be replaced by streaming at a later stage to make room for the late developers and to abolish the segmentation of the secondary system between the so-called academic and non-academic schools. Undoubtedly, this will be a step in the right direction, but that alone will not change the fundamental situation. Without more resources in the form of better equipped and better maintained schools, and the engagement of more highly trained teachers, the basic deficiencies are likely to remain, irrespective of the structures adopted.

The World Bank and the Caribbean Development Bank (CDB) are supporting projects in several countries to reform the basic education system. For example, several such projects are being developed in the member countries of the OECS. St Lucia is the first country to get off the ground with a project targeted on increasing access at the secondary level. The project provides, *inter alia*, for additional space, improved teacher training and curriculum development. Major projects are also underway in two of the larger Caribbean Community (CARICOM) countries.

One issue in educational reform is sustainability. This is not the first time that international assistance is being provided for improving the educational systems in the region. The outcome of past projects has been mixed; some improvements have seen sustainable results, while other initiatives have petered out. Financial constraints, poor management and loss of teachers continue to be among the factors affecting sustainability.

An area of particular concern is technical and vocational education. Over the past twenty years, a number of projects have been undertaken to increase access and improve quality. But the limited impact of these endeavours is seen by the annual output of technologists, technicians and skilled manual workers, which represents only a minuscule proportion of the labour force. Available data, though somewhat outdated and fragmentary, suggest that the annual output of such trained personnel is substantially less than 1 percent of the workforce. These data are reinforced by the multiplicity of reports of the continuing shortage of skilled workers in sectors such as manufacturing, construction and services.

Private Schools

In nearly every Caribbean country, private education plays an important role, especially in supplementing the instruction provided in government schools. This is most common in the form of private classes in preparation for the entrance and school-leaving examinations at the secondary level and in commercial skills training.

No systematic evaluations are available about the quality of private education. Much of private education is being provided by the teachers employed in the government schools and by retired teachers. It can therefore be assumed that it is not significantly inferior to the quality of instruction in grant-assisted schools.

A good case can be made for encouraging the expansion and upgrading of the private system provided it does not lead to resources diversion from the public system and a reduction of access for low-income students. As will be suggested later in this paper, private schools can play a useful role in the export of educational services.

Ideally, if the management of the school system becomes increasingly community based and cost sharing emerges as a regular feature of the system, the dichotomy between public and private schools could eventually disappear. At present, private tuition represents a distortion of the system, arising from the shortage of places, large classes and curriculum deficiencies.

The integration of the two systems could allow for productivity-related compensation and rewards for enterprise that can be beneficial to both teachers and students.

At present, no government in the region has a well-articulated policy towards private schools. The growth of private schools has been haphazard, and little monitoring of their performance takes place. It is therefore advisable that a more systematic approach be adopted with regard to private schools.

The Tertiary System

It was mentioned earlier that the principal problem at the tertiary level is one of access. Both governments and institutions agree that deliberate efforts must be made to increase access over the rest of the decade into the next century. Thus, UWI's Development Plan for the 1990s targeted a 50 percent increase in enrolments from 12,000 students in 1990 to 18,000 in 2000. However, this year (1994/95), enrolments have already reached approximately 17,500, and some faculties have exceeded their targeted increases.

The demand for tertiary education is essentially market-driven and closely follows the availability of jobs and comparative levels of remuneration. Significant excess is seen in the demand for student places in areas such as engineering and management studies, while more traditional faculties like medicine and law continue to attract high levels of applications. Spare capacity exists in the humanities, and even in the sciences – although capacity may be augmented in the sciences with the human and physical upgrading of the faculty that is now taking place. Particularly worrying are the small number of students in education and agriculture, reflecting students' perceptions of the poor career prospects in these fields.

Cost and Returns in Tertiary Education

Although it is generally acknowledged that economic development requires a significant expansion in the number of tertiary graduates, there is concern about the resource implications because of the high cost of UWI *vis-à-vis* other parts of the system and also in relation to some universities in other developing areas.

While there are many areas where UWI, like comparable institutions in the region and outside of the region, needs to be vigilant in pursuing cost economies, other considerations should be taken into account. For example, given the weaknesses in the primary and secondary system, a UWI education may be too cheap rather than too expensive. It is not known whether similar analogies can be drawn about some of the institutions with which UWI tends to be compared.

Universities today have to be viewed in international terms. In an era when international competitiveness is the guiding force for economic development, the quality of university graduates has to be comparable on an international scale. One of UWI's greatest strengths is the international recognition that is accorded to its degrees by overseas universities and professional bodies. Inevitably, this means that unit costs, while somewhat below those of the top universities, will tend to be higher than the other parts of the local educational system which do not have to satisfy tests of international competitiveness.

In the end, what matters are comparative returns from different types of education which essentially are the expected rates of "profitability" deriving from educational investment at different levels. International data, including information on Latin America and the Caribbean, strongly suggest that rates of return at the primary and secondary levels are much higher than those at the tertiary level.

Such data, while useful, should be interpreted with caution. They are usually not sufficiently disaggregated as between types of education at the different levels and do not take account of quality differences and externalities. For instance, some available information shows that rates of return on tertiary graduates in science and technology exceed those of graduates in other fields, as well as those of some secondary graduates, principally because science and technology graduates tend to be among the highest paid.

Again, the data do not usually distinguish between different levels of attainment by graduates in a particular field. Tracer studies indicate significant earning differentials between graduates according to the classes of their degrees.

Regarding externalities, academic staff employed in the university are expected to engage in research, including R&D, which could yield significant income streams over time for the researchers themselves and organizations that use the research.

Research

As the only institution of higher education of its kind in the region, UWI is seen as providing leadership in these fields. Almost since its establishment, UWI has sought to investigate local problems with an eye on their wider significance. This is illustrated by the success achieved in developing techniques to reverse mental retardation in malnourished children; in the record built up by a Medical Research Council (MRC) Unit on the Mona Campus in the clinical investigation of Sickle Cell anaemia. The MRC is currently researching the relationship between the Human T-cell leukaemia virus type 1 (HTLV-1) and leukaemia. Other faculties are also excelling in areas such as natural products, plant biotechnology, linguistics, early childhood and multicultural education, heritage studies, poverty and social policy, to name just a few. If UWI is to discharge its responsibilities as a focal point for enhanced research and R&D efforts, it has to have the capability to retain and attract scholars of international standing and participate in regional and international research networks.

Distance Education

Notwithstanding the quality and related cost pressures originating from the objective of attaining international competitiveness, UWI and the tertiary system as a whole should exploit any opportunities for lower cost expansion such as distance education. The university has been operating for over ten years a distance teaching project, principally serving the territories that do not have campuses. A development programme financed by the CDB is underway to increase the number of site stations, expand the levels and types of programmes delivered and improve the technology.

Distance education is particularly well suited to the dispersed community that the UWI serves. It will also facilitate cooperation with other universities, especially those in the wider Caribbean, thereby diversifying and strengthening outreach, teaching and research.

A well-articulated distance education system can serve not only the tertiary system but also the primary and secondary schools to make up for deficiencies in the quality and range of programmes. This has reinforced the point made earlier concerning the high priority that should be attached to training and re-training teachers and teacher-trainers in education technology.

Networking

One of the major trends in higher education today is the creation of networks and consortia of universities and related institutions on a local, regional and global scale. These are responses to the drive for global competitiveness and the establishment of new divisions of labour between institutions. It is likely that this trend will be accentuated in the period ahead, as both teaching and research become more globalized.

UWI is already associated with this trend. The Mona Campus of the University is currently delivering an Executive Master's in Public Sector Management, targeted towards students from small developing countries, with a teaching team consisting of local faculty and others drawn from four institutions in Australia, Britain and the United States. Consideration is currently being given to an invitation to join an international network of medical schools in the United Kingdom, France, Eastern Europe, Japan, Hong Kong and South Africa.

The network will provide for student and faculty exchanges and joint research. Within the Caribbean Basin itself, the European Union is funding a project to deliver eight bilingual master's degrees in a joint arrangement with three universities in the Dominican Republic and with a Haitian university coming on stream as soon as circumstances allow.

Cooperation arrangements are in place or being developed with about twenty universities in the United States, five leading Canadian universities and a score of universities in Britain. Most of these arrangements are cross-disciplinary and provide for student and faculty collaboration.

Additionally, some other universities have also begun to send students to UWI on a study-abroad basis.

Exports of Educational Services

One of the spin-offs from networking is the scope that it provides for exporting education services, not only to partner institutions locally but regionally and globally. Indeed, joint exporting to third countries is already being discussed as a feature of some existing cooperation arrangements.

An aspect of education exports is summer programmes, which are attractive enough to be marketed to international students. Educational tourism is growing worldwide. The Caribbean is well placed to add education to its "sun, sand and sea", in diversifying the tourism product.

One form of educational exports is educational franchising, whereby universities can license other institutions to deliver programmes with its certification. Given the tendency towards high re-location costs, students in some countries are already beginning to opt for local programmes delivered under the imprint of high-quality institutions. UWI is already receiving enquiries about its willingness to export programmes under such an arrangement.

A further component of educational exports is consultancy. The growth of international consultancy has opened up opportunities for universities to become competitive providers of consultancy services. Faculties at UWI are encouraged to undertake consultancy work for institutions and companies at national, regional and international levels. The university itself is now actively considering the establishment of an institution-wide consultancy facility. Already, approval has been given for the establishment of institutes in the Faculties of Medicine and Engineering that will, *inter alia*, provide consultancy services. Recently, UWI organized joint ventures with two Canadian universities to undertake consultancies relating to health and physical infrastructure.

Potential also exists for education exports at the secondary level. During the 1950s and 1960s, sizeable numbers of Latin American students, particularly from Colombia and Venezuela, attended schools in Jamaica, Barbados, and Trinidad and Tobago to receive a secondary school education in English. Some of this continues on a limited scale. With the shift towards free secondary education, student places for foreign students are no longer easy for them to obtain. Governments need to re-think their policies towards private secondary schools since these schools may be able to attract a flow of foreign secondary students. An additional source of students might also come from the families of Caribbean nationals abroad.

The Financing of Education

Caribbean countries are grappling with the problem, now almost universal, of allocating their scarce public resources among the competing demands of the different parts of the educational system. Although individual countries have not all made comprehensive policy statements on the matter, the present trend seems to be giving greater priority to primary and secondary education over tertiary, in the allocation of public funds.

Accordingly, top priority to primary education is justified on the grounds of equity, whereby public resources are directed towards the poorest children in the community. As one moves up the educational ladder, it is assumed that the students in the lowest income brackets will become a diminishing proportion of the total.

However, this does not mean that significant numbers of students in the lowest income brackets do not make it into the tertiary system. For example, a study done a few years ago show that 40 percent of the students at the Mona Campus of UWI came from families that were below the poverty line. A fruitful line of research would be to investigate the survival strategies which low-income students employ to maintain themselves in the tertiary system.

Given the shortage of resources set against expanding educational needs, non-governmental financing of education has become a pertinent issue. It is accepted in some countries that cost sharing, which is charging students a low percentage of the total tuition fees, should take place at the tertiary level. Thus UWI introduced in 1993 new tuition fees computed at 15 percent of the economic cost. All of the contributing countries to UWI, with the exception of The Bahamas and Barbados, require their students to pay the new scale of fees. The students from these two countries continue to receive free university education. Of note, recently, the University of Guyana also introduced fees.

Jamaica has gone further than the other countries in introducing fees throughout the tertiary system and in secondary schools. The fees charged in the secondary system are expected to cover non-salary operating costs, thus enabling the government to pay only salaries.

The new scale of fees was established with the expectation that governments would arrange for students to have greater access to student loans. So far, Jamaica and Trinidad and Tobago have made arrangements with their local commercial banks to provide student loans, but it is uncertain how long these arrangements will remain in force. Students in the OECS are experiencing special difficulties because of the very limited loan facilities existing in their countries. Further efforts have to be made to ensure sustainable arrangements in the countries where loan facilities have been introduced and to enlarge these facilities on a limited basis, pre-dating the introduction of the new fees.

In addressing these issues, a number of connected matters will require examination. These include the repayment terms of the loan, special arrangements for students coming from poor families who cannot provide guarantors, and whether special repayment terms can be offered to students who opt for employment after graduation in jobs with high social returns such as teaching and the public service. Fortunately, there exist many best practice examples in other countries, on which the Caribbean can usefully draw, in enlarging and improving student loan facilities.

Income Generation

Beyond tuition fees, the educational institutions, especially UWI, should become more active in income generation. Earlier reference was made to possibilities such as attracting international students, as well as contract research and consultancy. Additionally, systematic attention should be given to fund-raising from the alumni, the private sector, foundations, individual benefactors and the public at large. UWI is now becoming active in this area and hopes to expand its activities in the near future. Other institutions are also making efforts to mobilize resources from alumni and the organization of special events.

In consideration of the above, UWI and other educational institutions should become more entrepreneurial in character and adapt their institutional structures, their management methods and their policies to successfully contend with the new environment. This is no easy matter since at stake is the transformation of well-entrenched cultures. Universities worldwide can no longer be content with building reputations as high-quality centres of reflection. They need to take aggressive steps to attract students, satisfy their customers with marketable programmes and courses and win research and consultancy contracts. By these and other means, they can maximize their earnings, enabling them to recruit high-powered staff and to procure up-to-date equipment and plant. Institutions that fail to measure up to these standards are likely to be left behind. There are expectations that UWI will blaze a trail that can serve as a model for the rest of the tertiary system and the educational sector at large.

Management Reforms

Apart from the lack of entrepreneurial capacity, education systems in the region suffer from several management shortcomings. The most important of these is a high degree of centralization. Ministries of Education, often at the highest level, are involved in making decisions about comparatively minor matters. Over the years, the system has become heavily bureaucratized with little discretionary authority, and hence accountability, at the level of school principals.

Most of the problems identified in schools, that is, poor maintenance of the plant, sub-optimal utilization of places, inefficiencies in staff recruitment, materials and equipment procurement and weak linkages with the community, can be traced to centralization.

Many governments appear to be making a strong case for decentralization, and some of them have taken steps to delegate authority over specific matters to regional and community bodies. At the same time, interest is growing among the private sector, religious groups and civic groups such as service clubs, in providing support largely to individual schools. This provides a good basis for confidence-building among the public and private sectors.

School boards, Parent Teachers Associations and alumni groups are beginning to play a role in day-to-day management, but they are still essentially secondary actors. As the interplay between governments and communities increases, it should become feasible to move towards a community-based system of management, thereby relieving the government of the necessity to retain those responsibilities.

Ministries of Education can progressively concentrate on policy formulation, planning, standard-setting, and monitoring and evaluation. This will allow them to develop a strong research and analytical capacity to keep fully abreast of educational developments in the world and adapt them to local use. They will also be better equipped to operate early warning systems, spotting emerging problems and taking timely action to deal with them.

The complex problems that exist in school systems require a high degree of creativity and innovation to be successfully tackled. Other norm-setting institutions such as the family and the church seem to be losing ground. The school should try to make up the deficit through the active involvement of the community in diagnosing behavioural and learning problems, and in building motivation, teamwork and discipline.

In past periods, community institutions – mainly the church – were instrumental in the development of the educational system, partly because of the moral authority they exerted. In the difficult economic, social and human situation now prevailing in all Caribbean countries, it is to everyone's benefit that all interests contribute to the development of the educational system.

The Role of the Public Sector

Implicit in the above discussion is a significantly changing role for governments in the educational sector. They can be envisaged as increasingly divesting their responsibility for the management of the school system by encouraging the development of representative community bodies to take over the running of individual schools or schools in particular areas. A suggestion is that governments should establish national education foundations which would have overall responsibilities for arranging and overseeing the management of schools through building a network of community organizations.

As far as financing is concerned, one model could be for governments to provide full financing for primary education, the salary bill for secondary education and a significant portion (diminishing over time) of the economic cost per student for tertiary education.

Governments should also work towards the rationalization and progressive integration of public and private education to ensure equivalence in costs and standards while leaving space for entrepreneurial initiative.

The role of the government will not be diminished but will be different. That role would concentrate on planning and policy development, the setting of standards, ensuring adequate monitoring and reporting, keeping a watchful eye over the adequacy of resources available to the system as a whole, and ensuring that the public resources provided are used consistent with the overall strategy for educational development.

In general, the educational system should be the mirror image of what the society itself wants to achieve – a level playing-field, high productivity, efficiency and cost effectiveness in resource use, enterprise and innovation with commensurate private and social benefits.

Regional Cooperation

Education has for a long time been regarded as an area well suited for regional cooperation. The UWI and the Caribbean Examinations Council are often quoted as two successful examples in this field.

The principal justification for regional cooperation in education is the increasing need for achieving critical mass in expertise, information and management as the acquisition, generation and utilization of knowledge are contingent upon an increasing range of complex intellectual and technical activities. The Caribbean countries stand a lesser chance of building adequate institutional capacity on their own than if they cooperated.

Intriguing questions have been posed. Would it not be more efficient for very small countries to concentrate on providing primary and secondary education and import their higher education needs by sending their students abroad? Should they rely upon external providers to deliver education locally?

It is self-evident that the Caribbean should not aim at self-sufficiency in higher education. Instruction and research services are needed in a wide variety of fields where capital and recurrent outlays for equipment and specialized staff are well beyond the slender resources of the countries of the region.

However, it is unduly pessimistic to conclude that the region should rely principally upon overseas providers of higher education. Among other reasons, such a reliance would increase the likelihood of students permanently migrating to the places from which they received their education. More fundamentally, however, without the development of an indigenous knowledge base, the possibilities for meaningful participation in the global economy would be limited.

Without a local flow of well-trained graduates and a capacity for quality research and development, the investment and export prospects of the region would be poor.

Maintaining a strong regional university favours the decentralization of as much education and training as possible, to the widely dispersed localities in the region. Students will be able to minimize the amount of time that they need to spend on campuses. As previously observed, the use of the distance mode could reduce costs significantly.

Experience has shown that a strong regional university can help develop leadership in the arena of education, ranging all the way from teacher training, curriculum development, teaching materials and the operation of appropriate school examination systems. This does not imply rigid conformity among the different school systems. Rather, there are opportunities for experimentation and diversity with the benefits that would come from sharing experiences among different schools and countries.

The regional university has also performed well in producing government and private sector leaders. This is illustrated by the fact that seven of the current serving Heads of Government and numerous Ministers of Government are UWI graduates. UWI alumni are also to be found among the top management of companies and are dominant in the professional groups, in the media and in the leadership of some of the trade unions. Truly, it can be said that UWI has been doing its job of developing a cadre of local leaders, educated within a local setting, and fully conversant with the circumstances and potential of the area to which they belong.

Chapter 1.3

Education in the West Indies

Address to the Canadian International Development
Agency – CIDA, November 1989

President, Vice Presidents, Staff Members of CIDA, I feel privileged to share with you a few preliminary thoughts on education in the West Indies.

It is common knowledge that in many West Indian countries, the education system is regarded as being in a state of crisis. These countries are by no means in a unique situation. There are many developing countries today, especially the heavily indebted ones, where the twin forces of rapid population growth and public expenditure cuts are resulting in serious deterioration of educational standards. There are also developed countries such as the United States and Canada and developed nations in Europe, where complaints about falling standards are legion. The problem is clearly not only one of money, although more money for education is a necessary condition for achieving improvements.

West Indian governments need to realize that they are not the only ones in a stew. In terms of conventional indicators such as enrolment ratios, literacy rates and pass rates at the primary and secondary levels, they are not among the worst cases. Indeed, some of them such as Barbados and Trinidad and Tobago are among the best cases. Taking the area as a whole, gross enrolment ratios at the primary level are 90 percent and more, and at the secondary level well over 50 percent. Where the principal deficiency exists is at the tertiary level. The tertiary level enrolment in Jamaica and Trinidad and Tobago was 4 percent in 1986 when the average for middle income developing countries was between 17 and 18 percent. One should not, however, conclude that the educational problem is simply a tertiary one, since all levels of the system are inter-connected and deficiencies at one level can be traced to weaknesses at other levels.

Before speaking about the problems in the educational system, let me qualify what I have said about the comparative situation in the West Indies. Although our problems are not among the worst, there are special reasons why the situation in this area needs to be urgently addressed.

First, the West Indies has always faced a serious imbalance between population and resources, reflected in the fact that population densities are among the highest in the world. Accordingly, the quality of human input into economic development has always been viewed as being of prime importance. However, in the vast majority of countries, economic growth has to date been managed to create commensurate employment opportunities for the growing labour force.

Jamaica is perhaps the worst case in the area where rates of open unemployment have, by and large, remained over the past four decades at 20 percent and above. Some of the other islands have experienced short bursts of high employment, notably Trinidad and Tobago during the petroleum boom in the 1970s and Antigua at the present time. But as a broad generalization, open unemployment has persisted at high rates throughout most of the region, especially during the recession and adjustment conditions of the 1980s.

If CARICOM countries are to be more successful in resolving the unemployment problems, greater efforts must be made to educate and train the population for productive employment.

A second reason why education deserves top priority involves the need to change the structure of the economies. The traditional sectors have limited potential for future growth, especially staples such as sugar and bananas. Petroleum reserves in Trinidad and Tobago are close to exhaustion, with bauxite in Jamaica being only two or three decades behind. Although tourism may be capable of sustained buoyancy, one should not take it for granted.

All of the CARICOM countries have to search earnestly for new sources of growth in the 1990s. This will involve modernization and diversification of the agricultural sector, developing the manufacturing sector beyond its rudimentary stage, upgrading tourism and entering new lines of service production, all of which require greater knowledge and skills intensity. The computer revolution, now radically transforming processes and techniques of production in practically every sector of the economy, adds further cogency to this requirement.

A third factor that gives the education problem special significance in the Caribbean is the high rate of external migration, especially among skilled and professional people. Given the particularly close ties which prevail between the West Indies and North America, it is to be assumed that a net loss of people to the United States and Canada will continue for some time to come. Accordingly, the West Indies have to educate and train more persons than would otherwise be required to meet the domestic needs of economic development.

On economic grounds alone, there should therefore be no complacency in tackling the problem of the educational system. I shall not go into the non-economic reasons such as the role of education as an agent of social mobility and social progress and for improving people participation in development and democratic processes. Education can also help to address social problems such as drug addiction and communicable diseases. Education is also a vital factor in combating the environmental degradation that is becoming a burning issue in this region.

Educational Problems to Be Addressed

The principal educational and knowledge problems that the West Indies need to address can be reduced to five:

1. The poor quality of pre-school, primary and secondary education reflected in low examination pass rates in subjects such as English, mathematics and science. The bulk of school leavers lack the cognitive and numerical skills that are necessary for successful entry into the job market. The inadequate performance of primary and secondary schools is attributable to shortages of trained teachers and educational materials, as well as ill-maintained physical plants.

2. The limited opportunities available for acquiring an industrial or technical skill. Accordingly, one finds that in Jamaica, of the 203,000 persons reported as unemployed in 1988, 89 percent of them had received no formal training. At the same time, only about 4 percent of the relevant cohort is enrolled in a technical or vocational school.

3. Quantitative and qualitative deficiencies in tertiary education. As far as tertiary enrolment is concerned, the figure for Jamaica is about 5 percent compared with the average for middle income developing countries of 16 to 17 percent. The situation is particularly acute in science and technology. I often quote the case of Singapore – admittedly a special one, where with a total population of 2.6 million, tertiary enrolment in science and technology is 18,000. Jamaica with a population of 2.4 million has about 1,800. The low percentage of engineering students in Jamaica is also of concern. Available data on newly industrialized countries in Latin America, South Asia and South East Asia shows that engineering students constitute between 20 and 40 percent of total tertiary enrolment. At UWI, we have 800 engineering students out of a total enrolment of 12,000 students.

4. A rudimentary knowledge base characterized by excessive dependence on imported technology, inadequate numbers of local scientists (at Mona, registrations in science have virtually remained static over the past 10 years at approximately 1,000), limited research and development activities and poor dissemination of research results.

5. Shortcomings in the management of educational and knowledge institutions. The management of the educational system is highly centralized in Ministries of Education, permitting only limited involvement in the operation of the schools by community and non-governmental groups such as churches. There are no special incentives to encourage private sector participation in the financing and management of the school system or in research and development.

Possible Elements towards a Solution

The problems of the educational system go beyond those listed above and are multi-faceted and complex. No one should pretend to have a complete solution to them. Nonetheless, certain lines of action, if well planned and implemented, are likely to meet with success. They include:

1. Remedial work and continuing education programmes for primary and secondary school teachers in English, mathematics and science. Given the geographical dispersion of the West Indian territories, distance teaching can play an important role in developing these programmes;

2. Major initiatives to increase technical and vocational education, tailored to specific occupations likely to be important in the economy, and with an orientation towards developing capability for self-employment;

3. Increasing access to tertiary education with a focus on science and technology and management disciplines to broaden opportunities for work/study programmes to improve the employability of graduates;

4. Collaborative efforts by governments and the private sector to fund research and development activities;

5. The decentralization of the education system to permit the community-based management of schools. Decentralization could bring benefits by way of more effective monitoring of performance, greater accountability and cost-effectiveness and greater recognition of teachers.

All of these will cost money at a time when most West Indian governments are under severe financial constraints. They are likely to remain in this situation into the 1990s. In terms of overall allocation to education, most governments are already devoting about 5 to 6 percent of their GNP that favourably compares with other countries, both developing and developed.

Undeniable scope exists for the more efficient use of resources. Governments may also consider re-allocating resources to favour primary, technical and vocational education. International studies show higher rates of return on primary education than on secondary or tertiary education. However, this is not intended to endorse simplistic propositions that countries should concentrate more on primary education and pay less attention to the other two levels. As I said before, one should recognize the close inter-connectedness between the different levels of the educational system. For instance, it is quite obvious that one cannot improve the supply and quality of primary and secondary school teachers without increasing access and upgrading quality at the tertiary level.

What emerges is that a truly national effort is required to improve the educational system, involving financial contributions from the state, the private sector and parents who can afford to do so. Among other things, this would facilitate the establishment of cost-recovery schemes at the secondary and tertiary levels. These are currently being studied by some governments in the area and also by the university.

Concluding Remarks

If the West Indies is to make the transition to high growth and greater international competitiveness during the 1990s, steps such as those I have outlined above will have to be taken in the immediate future. UWI is ready to play its part by improving its own performance and by working with governments and communities to upgrade the educational system as a whole. We simply cannot afford to fail.

Let me end with two caveats. There are no spontaneous forces which will transform an educated and skilled labour force into new economic activity. Without the emergence of vigorous entrepreneurship, and a policy environment favourable to increasing investment and production, countries could find themselves continuing along a path of surplus labour and external migration, even after they have upgraded the educational attainment of their labour force. Governments, therefore, should ensure that they maintain a good investment climate through appropriate macro- and micro-economic policies. Furthermore, better education is not necessarily synonymous with greater achievement. Low productivity can be found among the most highly educated people. Sir Arthur Lewis expressed this eloquently in the following quotation:

You must be willing to work hard while your companions are at play. You must be willing to practice over and over again, until you get it right. You must be highly self-critical. You must be humble enough to welcome, analyze and apply the criticism of others, or you will never learn. There is no doubt that achievers have a special type of personality. This drive for achievement is not identical with brain power. Many people with excellent brains achieve nothing, while men with moderate brains can be highly successful if they have the drive to achieve.

If we are to take full advantage of our human resources endowments, the West Indies has to develop a culture of production, to transform ourselves from talkers to doers. This could well be the most elusive task of all.

Chapter 1.4

Education and Training

The Keys to Survival of Developing Countries, Address to 9th World Conference on Cooperative Education at the Jamaica Pegasus Hotel, August 31, 1995

Mr Chairman, distinguished delegates, I am pleased indeed to be speaking at the session this morning. Before I make my substantive remarks, I wish to join members who have congratulated our host institution, the College of Arts, Science and Technology (CAST), which will be renamed the Polytechnic University of Jamaica. I congratulate its president, Dr Alfred Sangster.

Dr Sangster is a Caribbean giant in education, and we have become accustomed to receiving from him nothing but excellence.

This conference is already providing indications of becoming a landmark both for Jamaica and the Caribbean, and I hope for cooperative education throughout the world. We see everywhere the great interest that lies in the philosophy and approaches of cooperative education, which serve to bring the worlds of study and work closer. Cooperative education is therefore of the highest relevance to the economic and social progress of all countries, especially countries endeavouring to move beyond the stages of under-development.

In beginning my comments, I make two caveats. You have asked me to speak about developing countries, but I shall mainly confine my remarks to the English-speaking Caribbean, although much of what I will say is relevant to all of the Caribbean.

You have also asked me to speak about education and survival. It is interesting how the language of public dialogue about developing countries is changing. A decade ago, you would have asked me to speak about development. However, with the adverse changes and trouble spots emerging in many parts of the world, taken together with the new international environment now unfolding, expectations about the future are being lowered everywhere.

We ought to try and avoid being imprisoned in a new wave of pessimism. Given the depth and scale of the problems facing most developing countries, they are obligated to use every means at their disposal to chart a positive course and to achieve as much economic and social improvement as possible. I shall therefore take survival to mean steady, even if unspectacular economic growth, that would allow countries in the region to sustain improvements in living conditions and in the quality of life.

This confirms with the projections made for most countries in the English-speaking Caribbean which are targeting an average annual growth in their gross domestic product (GDP) of 3 percent for the remainder of the 1990s and the first decade of the 21st century. This is a comparatively modest performance that merely keeps the rate of economic growth ahead of the rate of population growth and is far less than was recorded in decades such as the 1960s when average annual rates of growth of 6 percent and more were not uncommon. But we live in such a different world today.

Jamaica and the rest of the Caribbean encounter daunting challenges, many of which have been accumulated over previous decades.

Development Challenges

The first is that the recent rates of growth have been rather unpromising, in the best cases slow, in others negative. After a decade or more of such unsatisfactory performance, it is a major task to turn around the economy and to achieve and sustain satisfactory rates for economic growth. It involves not only structural change but also a new policy environment and new attitudes.

Secondly, unemployment continues to be a major scourge in the region. Over the past few years, some improvements have occurred. For example, in Jamaica, the unemployment rate has dipped from around 22 to 23 percent to around 18 percent. This is good news, but 18 percent still represents an elevated high rate of unemployment. Similarly, in Trinidad and Tobago the rate of unemployment more than doubled over the 1980s, though the rate is decreasing again. In one way or another, all Caribbean countries should continue making employment creation and the reduction of unemployment key items of their policy agenda.

Thirdly, poverty continues to be an area of serious concern. It would appear from the data available that poverty increased over the last decade. It is not uncommon now to find that one-quarter or more of households are below the poverty line. We are encountering the phenomenon of the working poor, whereas hitherto poverty was uniquely associated with unemployment. Far too many of the new jobs being created are at the bottom of the scale in terms of wage levels and skills attainment.

Fourthly, practically all the Caribbean countries face severe problems of economic diversification. The traditional agricultural exports are losing ground. Sugar and bananas, which constitute the mainstay of the agricultural sector, face a most uncertain future. This is because of the distinct possibility that the special trade preferences on which they have depended for an extended period of time will be terminated due to pressure from competing countries or from countries with business interests in those countries.

It is a matter of the utmost urgency that every effort is made to find alternative lines of production that could provide comparable sources of employment and foreign exchange earnings. Some progress is being made in developing non-traditional agricultural exports such as exotic fruits and vegetables, horticulture and aquaculture, but these efforts are still on a relatively small scale.

Tourism has emerged as the major alternative and has become the leading earner of foreign exchange in the region and the largest source of employment. About one-quarter of the labour force in the region is currently engaged in activities relating to tourism.

Tourism should no longer be thought of as "sun, sand and sea". The range of tourist attractions is broadening, as evidenced by new types of tourism such as community tourism, heritage tourism, eco-tourism, health tourism and educational tourism. The present perception is to view tourism as an axial sector around which radiates a wide range of goods, production and services activities. One recent writer has estimated that over fifty services activities are directly or indirectly linked to tourism. The present task is to build up a broadly based tourism sector offering a range of culturally and environmentally friendly attractions to cater to visitors from different countries and age groups.

Tasks Facing the Educational System

Given the tasks that I have just described, it is incumbent upon the educational system to take the lead in meeting many of the new requirements for skills and for building leadership capacity. It is widely recognized that substantial reform of the educational system is required, if it is to be more supportive of the development needs of the region.

A major area of reform is to improve the employability of school leavers from primary and secondary schools. Too high a proportion of students leave those schools without the basic cognitive and numerical skills required in the workplace. Complaints are widespread about the large number of students who leave primary schools and even secondary schools as semi-literates.

Governments recognize that they should address this problem with great urgency. The contemporary world demands that students acquire job-specific skills and generic skills such as problem-solving and teamwork. Indeed, many educators believe that significant progress will not be made in employability until the entire primary and secondary school systems are computerized so that students will leave school as computer literates.

In Caribbean terms, this is an arduous task involving enormous capital outlays. One commentator suggested recently that the initial capital expenditure for computerization in the region could well run into US$1 billion. But computerized school systems will also involve widespread training and re-training of teachers and developing maintenance capacity for servicing the equipment installed in the school system. To date, many schools in the region do not even have a single computer, so it is a tall order indeed, to move from the present situation to full computerization.

Yet, we should not mistake the difficult for the impossible. The costs of computer hardware and software are trending downwards so that the acquisition of hardware and software will probably become increasingly more feasible with the passage of time. I shall mention later that a truly national effort is required to mobilize the resources for transforming the school system without complete reliance on the government's budget.

A further broad area for educational reform is to increase the output of graduates from the tertiary system. The Caribbean is quite distinctive with its low tertiary enrolment ratio. The average for the region is just under 5 percent compared with a figure of 16 to 17 percent for middle income developing countries taken as a whole. This low percentage cannot foster economic growth and development.

Further investigation shows a dire situation in terms of the output of technicians and technologists. The World Bank has estimated that in every country in the region, the annual output of graduates at the industrial craft level is less than 1 percent of the labour force. These are the persons who constitute the backbone of a modern economy. At the university level, the output of graduates in science and technology is still unsatisfactory compared with the situation in rapidly growing countries.

The University of the West Indies (UWI) and the tertiary system are mindful of these deficiencies and are working purposefully to remedy them in the shortest possible time.

Resources

The improvements in the educational system involve more resources, both of money and people. The Caribbean countries made good strides in increasing the resources devoted to education over the 1960s and 1970s, but because of the poor growth performance in the 1980s, the resources allocated to education decreased. In previous decades, most countries were spending about 5 percent of their gross national product (GNP) and 20 percent of their government budget on education. Although some exceptions exist today, the respective figures are presently closer to 3.5 percent and 13 to 14 percent. As I have already pointed out, with the modest economic growth that is projected, it is most unlikely that more public resources will be available for education over the rest of the decade.

It is also recognized that the private sector has a major role to play in assisting schools financially. Some companies are now adopting individual schools, offering bursaries and scholarships, sometimes with vacation employment attached and contributing to fundraising efforts. We see a revival of interest in apprenticeship schemes. In general, the private sector today has a much stronger perception of its own interests in a good education system than it had some years before.

It is the task of the educational institutions themselves to broaden their constituencies of support among individuals and organizations with the capacity to contribute. This implies active alumni and fundraising programmes and other initiatives. Institutions should increasingly recognize their obligation to find themselves some of the funds for their operations. This requires attitudes of entrepreneurship and initiative on the part of the leadership, the staff, the parents and the students. Together, they need to make the goal of development their own and convince the rest of the community of the legitimacy of their claims.

At the tertiary level, there are special opportunities that may be grasped for income generation. It should be the objective of all institutions to establish profit centres in their operations. One of particular interest is the field of contract research and consultancy, whereby institutions can sell their services to the private and public sectors, at home, within the region and internationally.

Institutions are developing their research and consultancy services in partnership with institutions overseas and fostering networking arrangements with them. The reality is that higher education is becoming increasingly globalized, and institutions will need to be internationally competitive to function successfully at home and in the international market.

The task is enormous. We should view survival and growth not only in terms of the national and regional needs for development but also in terms of the opportunities to compete internationally. At UWI, we are fully aware of the challenges involved in competing at the local, regional and international levels but we are finding that with determination, we are beginning to move ahead in some fields.

I turn finally to the wider role that education plays in social engineering. We have learned over these past decades that survival and progress are not about bread alone. There is an increasing awareness about the need to protect our ecology and to correct patterns of deviant behaviours such as crime, violence and drug use that threaten the social fabric of our nations.

The fragility of the ecologies of the Caribbean is illustrated by the situation in the sister island of Montserrat, with some 15,000 inhabitants, which up to a few days ago was threatened by the twin disasters of a volcanic eruption and a hurricane. Fortunately, the situation is now less threatening, although the volcanic hazard still needs to be carefully monitored.

In other countries in the region, we see increasing evidence of land erosion, deforestation, water pollution, damaged beaches, destruction of the coral reefs, all of which require urgent and continuing attention. The education and training of personnel in environmental management and the spread of environmental education throughout the system, and the society at large, have become top priorities.

The issue of the environment is part of the wider problem of social sustainability. Like so many other countries in the world – large and small, rich and poor – we see a great need to protect the social order from the perversions of crime and other forms of deviant behaviours. Every nation in the world is being challenged to find new answers to today's social problems.

If education is to serve its full purpose of strengthening society, it should be the vehicle for greater enlightenment, understanding and cooperation. In our increasingly interdependent world, an ethos and ethics of cosmopolitanism must be developed so that people of different wealth and income, races, cultures and perceptions can live together harmoniously. Our educational institutions are obligated to play a leading role in building the new ethos and ethics within institutions and between them and help to further the process in the wider society and world.

All that I have been saying means that educational institutions should develop new sources of dynamism and innovation if they are to respond adequately to the needs of the present and the future.

This topic returns me to my original thoughts about cooperative education. I have been speaking about relevance, cost-sharing, international competitiveness, social cohesion and international understanding – which is of importance to all of us. I do hope that the cooperative approach can grow, not only in Jamaica and the Caribbean but also in other developing countries as we attempt to respond to the formidable challenges that lie ahead.

I thank you.

Chapter 1.5

Deficiencies in Education

Thwarting Regional Development: Article Published in the Sunday Gleaner, March 8, 1992

Complaints about the educational system in Jamaica and in several other Caribbean countries are now legion. Chronic shortage of qualified teachers, deteriorating buildings and equipment and shortage of materials are among the most pervasive problems. The poor quality of the educational system is largely a phenomenon of the 1970s and 1980s. In the decades before the 1970s, Jamaica and the rest of the region had a reputation for good education.

A high percentage of the persons who occupied important positions in the post-war period only had a primary school education. During the colonial period and in the pre-independence years, Jamaica and Barbados, in particular, supplied teachers to English-speaking countries in West Africa. At the secondary level, some countries in the region exported educational services, taking students from nearby Latin American countries who wished to have a secondary school education in English. Sometimes these were the children of West Indian migrants who held a deep respect for the high standard of schooling in the region.

Although standards were high, the numbers that were educated were rather small. In 1950, the gross enrolment ratio in primary education in Jamaica was 68 percent, and secondary education 15 percent. Currently, the figures are approximately 100 percent at the primary level and over 50 percent at the secondary level. The rapid expansion in school populations started in the 1970s when the Government of Jamaica adopted a policy of free secondary education. During the 1980s, the effective implementation of this policy was constrained by decreasing public expenditure on education which had the effect of reducing standards. Valued in constant 1974 dollars, the recurrent expenditure on education fell from a peak of $129 million in 1977–78 to a low of $93 million in 1984–85, and is reported to have reached an even further low in 1987–88.

In a Nutshell

To put the matter in a nutshell, the principal problem in primary and secondary education has become one of quality rather than quantity. In the case of the tertiary system, there are serious deficiencies in quantity, and in some cases in quality. At the quantitative level, the gross enrolment rate in Jamaica is no more than 6 percent or about one-third of the average for middle income developing countries.

I often cite the case of Singapore – admittedly a special one – which has a population not too dissimilar to Jamaica (2.6 million as against 2.4) but has about ten times the number of students enrolled at the tertiary level in science and technology. Also compare the regional picture in relation to engineering. The so-called newly industrializing countries have a range of 20 percent to 40 percent of their post-secondary students enrolled in engineering studies. At the University of the West Indies (UWI), some 800 engineering students are enrolled out of a total enrolment in all faculties of almost 12,000.

In the natural sciences, it is a matter of concern to note that in the ten-year period between 1977–78 and 1987–88, there was virtually no growth in the number of students registered for a first degree at the Mona Campus. The numbers remained almost static at just over 1,000 although there was a small increase in the number of postgraduate students.

Virtually no growth has been recorded in the intake of students into the natural sciences at Mona because of inadequate preparation at the secondary level in mathematics and science. This inadequate preparation is also manifested in the high failure rate in preliminary and introductory courses in subjects such as mathematics and computer sciences. In 1987–88, the failure rate for the preliminary course in mathematics was 37 percent, and in the introductory course, the failure rate was 40 percent. In computer science, the failure rate in the introductory course was 35 percent. I have been drawing illustrations from university education in discussing deficiencies in the tertiary system, but one should not confuse the two.

The University Is Only One Part of the Tertiary System

The university is only one part of the tertiary system. Tertiary education refers to the whole range of post-secondary education, including the College of Arts, Science and Technology (CAST), technical and vocational colleges and schools, community colleges, teacher training colleges, agricultural training institutions and work/study schemes often involving formal apprenticeships.

Some of the commentaries on the deficiencies in tertiary education in the area of science and technology have missed this distinction and have erroneously argued that the training of technicians is of a higher priority than the training of scientists. The training needs of the two categories are complementary rather than competitive. Scientists and engineers require technicians in order to do their work. The reverse also applies.

At UWI, significant progress has been made in recent years in making admission requirements flexible. Thus, it is now possible to secure entry by passing the University of Cambridge or the University of London Ordinary Levels into degree programmes in natural sciences and in arts, offered in the evenings, as against passing the University of Cambridge or University of London Advanced Levels. It is also possible to secure partial or full accreditation for a number of diploma and certificate programmes offered by other tertiary institutions, thereby reducing the time students are required to complete a degree.

Students at the Sir Arthur Lewis Community College in St Lucia and the Antigua State College can now pursue the first year of the degree work in arts, sciences and social sciences. This opportunity will be extended to other tertiary level institutions as circumstances permit. The Bachelor of Education degree is now being offered by special arrangements with the Mico Teacher Training College in Jamaica, the College of The Bahamas and most recently at the Sir Arthur Lewis College.

The central issue facing the upgrading and enlargement of the educational system in Jamaica, and to some extent in other Caribbean countries, is finding the resources to make the necessary changes. There is limited room available to governments for increasing expenditure on education.

Typical Case

In the typical case, the government is already devoting 5 percent to 6 percent of gross national product (GNP) to expenditure on education, which compares well with developed countries and other developing countries at similar levels of development. It can be argued that Jamaica can modestly increase the proportion of its national budget devoted to education, from the present level of about 13 percent, and bring it close to the average for middle income developing countries, which is 15 percent to 16 percent. But this may not involve any absolute increase in expenditure since the government, in any event, is expected to constrain the growth in overall public expenditure to keep the budget deficit within acceptable proportions. Prospects for revenue growth are also at best, modest, since it is unlikely that the economy itself will achieve anything but small increments of growth in the short term.

Given this set of circumstances, the potential for improving educational systems will depend on several factors. The achievement of greater cost-effectiveness in education is vital so that greater value is received for money spent. Also of urgency is the ability of the government to concentrate available resources on the areas of greatest need, of which the upgrading of primary education is first on the list: and the readiness and the ability of private sources to take up the slack at other levels.

In other words, we have reached a situation in Jamaica and in most of the English-speaking Caribbean where free education at the secondary and tertiary levels is no longer feasible. If we wish to continue to have free education at these levels, we shall have to accept a deterioration in standards. The demands of economic development under present conditions make free higher education an unrealistic choice.

Economic development is about choices. Parents, especially those in the middle- and upper-income categories, have to decide what importance to assign to education in their household expenditure. They will have to decide what priority to give education as against, say, investment in other items, such as motor cars, satellite dishes, other state-of-the-art appliances and equipment. This will ordinarily involve parents and their children, who are direct beneficiaries of these levels of education, assuming full or partial responsibility for the cost of their education. Modalities will have to be found for expanding student loan schemes and student employment opportunities during vacations.

Ability to Pay

An approach to the financing of education along these lines combines both principles of equity and ability to pay. By providing for the full public financing of an improved system of primary education, it ensures that all students, irrespective of their parents' income, will receive a sound educational foundation. At the same time, the new approach would require households to contribute to the cost of higher levels of education on terms that take into account their ability to pay.

The root of the problem is that the UWI and the tertiary system as a whole in Jamaica, and indeed the entire Caribbean, is too small to fulfil the development needs of the region.

The true situation is that at the moment, there is only a 2 percent probability that a Jamaican student can get into university. The figures for nearly all of the other contributing countries are not much better. This, to my mind, is unsustainable – both from the point of view of the development of the country and from the point of view of the legitimate aspirations of young West Indians to get the best education. So, far from any proposal for cost-sharing that may be made in the future to address the situation seen as being elitist – it is non-elitist. The university is planning a 50 percent increase in enrolments by the end of the decade and the real issue is – how that is to be financed. In my own view, it is no longer feasible, given the current economic and financial situation, for the governments of the Caribbean to bear the full cost of university expansion.

I say this after giving careful consideration to the facts of the case. The facts are that the substantial expansion that we require together with the need for refurbishing the facilities of the university that have deteriorated over the past twenty years or so present financial magnitudes that one cannot realistically expect Jamaica and other Caribbean countries to bear alone, over the next several years.

Borrowing Money

We are therefore obliged to borrow money. We have also to mobilize money from our alumni, the private sector and the community at large. We have to find ways and means to repay the funds. Furthermore, the university will be taking steps to increase its own income. We are planning a major increase in summer school programmes to attract not only students from the Caribbean but from outside the region as well. We are planning to increase our work in contract research through which we can earn consulting fees, and we shall resolutely pursue efforts to become more cost-effective. All of the staff – academic, administrative and those engaged in the support services – simply have to work harder if we are to respond adequately to the situation.

We are also examining the conditions under which we could have a more economic system of tuition fees. But we would not wish to introduce a system that defeats the objective of giving all young West Indians who are appropriately qualified, the chance of getting a university education. And that is not just an economic objective. It is a social objective as well. Education has been and continues to be the main vehicle for achieving greater mobility in our societies.

Chapter 1.6

New Directions in Education in the OECS Countries, Address to the Education Conference

St Lucia – May 29–31, 1990

Introduction

Let me say how pleased I am to speak at this National Consultation on Education. This meeting could not have been timelier. St Lucia, along with other OECS and Caribbean Community (CARICOM) states, must begin addressing the future requirements for sustaining and, where possible, increasing economic growth in the context of a rapidly changing world environment. It is best to start with an analysis and appraisal of the education system since knowledge has now become a central ingredient of economic and social progress. Today, I would like to make a few observations about new directions in education in the OECS countries.

Over the last few years, new directions in education have emerged. These developments have been influenced and sustained to a large extent by regional initiatives and developments such as the establishment of the Caribbean Examination Council (CXC), the continued activities of the University of the West Indies (UWI) and the CARICOM Secretariat and the establishment of the OECS Secretariat. Most recently, the Caribbean Development Bank (CDB) has shown an interest in educational matters other than student loans, which signals a direction welcomed by many. Apart from the regional institutions, assistance has been forthcoming from international donors and lending agencies such as USAID, Canadian International Development Agency (CIDA), UNESCO, Caribbean Network of Educational Innovation for Development (CARNEID), Organization of American States, among others.

These new directions in education have been seen at the pre-primary, primary, secondary and tertiary levels of the system. This is not to say that new directions have been entirely in the form of institutional development. We have also seen the establishment of new modes of delivery of programmes via distance teaching methods like UWIDITE. In many educational circles, it is considered that UWIDITE represents the area that is likely to have the greatest impact on the educational systems of the sub-region. The importance of distance teaching methods is underscored in a statement made by Professor Errol Miller (1987). He said: "to offset some of the problems encountered in providing teacher upgrading and training as well as primary and secondary education for expanding school populations, many developed and developing countries have found distance education to be an effective tool."[1]

Pre-primary Education

Starting at the pre-primary level, greater attention is now being paid to the provision of effective pre-school programmes in all OECS countries. Governments have become active in an area that is still mainly run by private bodies. The new emphasis is no doubt influenced by the awareness that children's intellectual growth depends to a large extent on what happens to them between two to five years of age. Every care should be taken to provide the right context and conditions which will nurture the developing mind.

Primary Education

For many students, primary education still represents a terminal level. This fact has led to more focus on why we teach, what we teach, how we teach it and to what effect. Curricula have been developed in such core areas as mathematics, social studies, science and language arts. Curricula for primary school education are being enhanced both locally and regionally through the UWI/USAID Primary Education Project (1979–1985). These developments, through constant upgrading over the years, have produced knowledge and skills that are more in keeping with modern trends.

Many new directions are emerging in primary education. In language arts and reading, there is increasing emphasis on diagnosis of difficulties and remedial action. Where mathematics is concerned, there is a move to make the curriculum more classroom-focused, drawing heavily on community-based problems. In social studies, the trend is towards critical awareness of the symbols of nationhood, leading hopefully to new attitudes towards other individuals, the community, the nation and the region. Hopefully, this will instil in students a greater awareness of the processes of regional integration and closer unity that are currently being discussed.

In the area of science, many new features are emerging. There is a new thrust towards science education for scientific and technological literacy, with emphasis on knowledge of concepts and principles, the understanding of the nature of science and the application of scientific knowledge to everyday life. A more conscious effort to popularize science is evidenced by in-country and regional science fairs and the formation of science clubs. The curriculum is also increasingly introducing the inter-linkages between science, technology and society. For example, a major aim of the Primary Science Curriculum in St. Vincent and the Grenadines is "To sensitize children to the social implications involved in the use of Science". Science offerings also stress the importance of developing healthy attitudes towards the environment. The Antigua Primary Science Curriculum captures this environmental slant in one of its aims, which is "to develop desirable values and attitudes towards each other, the environment and the country". Some of its modules address health and safety, pollution and conservation, the use and misuse of drugs, and man and his environment.

In recent times there has also been a new philosophy and direction in technical education and vocational training. With external funding, the OECS countries have set up multi-island workshops offering four basic technical/vocational subject areas. The OECS countries seem to be using these strategically located centres to service the senior grades – of surrounding primary schools. The New World Bank/CDB multipurpose workshops are intended to serve the eleven to twenty-five age cohort in primary and secondary schools. Equipment and curricula for this latter initiative should be on site soon.

Secondary Education

Many of the new developments at the primary level continue into the secondary level. Here, the innovations in the Caribbean Examination Council (CXC) provide the underpinning for curriculum materials and practices that had begun at the primary level. A few points, however, bear elaboration. Secondary schools, which hitherto had seen the teaching of reading and elementary mathematics as the preserve of primary education, are now coming to the realization that they too should be involved. Many believe that this trend needs to be strengthened.

The proposed post-secondary certification by CXC should further influence developments at the secondary level.

Tertiary Education: Teacher Training

The problem of large numbers of untrained teachers in the various systems continues to militate against quality education.

Certain countries have attempted to train the backlog using in-service school-based models (National Inservice Teacher Programme (NISTEP in Grenada and Dominica)). Both attempts have not been as successful as anticipated, mainly because of the lack of proper infrastructure and planning. The danger is that rapid staff turnover – possibly engendered by poor pay and conditions of service – will continue in the foreseeable future, unless these challenges are addressed. All CARICOM countries should recognize that they cannot achieve further economic and social advancement in the conditions of today unless the educational system is revitalized through significant improvements in the salaries, conditions of service and status of our teachers.

Some new initiatives and directions are now in the planning stage. First, there is the project funded by CIDA and executed by the Organization for Cooperation in Overseas Development (OCOD). The target population in this project is the large numbers of teachers already in the system who have less than the four "O" Levels or CXC passes required for entry into Teachers' College. Secondly, there is the EDF-Funded Programme for training non-graduate secondary teachers in the OECS.

Both projects will use distance teaching techniques, probably administered at UWIDITE, but will also utilize print and audio materials. One should not underestimate the work done, since many in the target population have a history of poor study habits and morale.

Finally, one should recall that the tertiary system is expected to be the mainspring for high-level human resources development, contributing towards the pool of professional and para-professional skills. This is being achieved through:

(a) University-level programmes aimed at training more persons on a cost-effective basis;
(b) Training in non-traditional areas targeted towards specific manpower needs.

The CARICOM countries are still far behind in tertiary education, having on average a gross enrolment ratio of not more than 5%/6%, which is one-third of the average for middle-income developing countries. The situation with tertiary enrolments in science and technology is particularly perturbing.

This situation needs to be decisively tackled if economic development is not to be held back. There also needs to be enhanced efforts to train staff for tertiary-level institutions. Such staff development may be delivered through UWIDITE, summer courses and other short attachments on campus as well as through the regular on-campus programmes already in place at the university. There also needs to be greater flexibility regarding accreditation and certification – and fortunately, some overseas universities and colleges have already demonstrated their flexibility in this context.

At UWI, we are making conscious efforts to strengthen our links with other tertiary-level institutions. We are trying hard to mobilize resources for this purpose. In that connection, I am happy to say that the Government of Canada recently made a grant of CAN$10 million to the university. Part of that grant will be devoted to strengthening our work in education. This includes remedial programmes for teachers in English, mathematics and science. We are also strengthening educational administration, including school management and the multi-media production of teaching materials.

I end as I began by encouraging you to lift your sights to the future that lies ahead – full of uncertainties and challenges, but also full of opportunities. Let us from our different vantage points commit ourselves to the common cause of helping young St. Lucians and other young West Indians to take advantage of the opportunities that lie ahead.

Note

1. Miller, E. "Academic Upgrading of Unqualified Teachers in Windward Islands by Distance Teaching: Feasibility Study, 1987".

Chapter 1.7

Reflections on the Problem of Unemployment in the Commonwealth Caribbean the Commonwealth Caribbean into the Seventies

Proceedings of a Conference held at Howard University, Washington, D.C. on September 28–30, 1973

My understanding is that we are gathered at this conference to engage in stock-taking, to assess where we have reached in the Commonwealth Caribbean regarding unemployment. I understand that my terms of reference are to report on the question of unemployment, which is a major issue as unemployment affects nearly every area of economic policy. Accordingly, this paper serves merely as an introduction to unemployment and is not a definitive discussion of the subject.

Although unemployment has been the central economic and social problem of the Commonwealth Caribbean for this entire century, our knowledge of the problem leaves much to be desired. Apart from the decennial census, only one or two territories are making systematic attempts to gather information on the subject with greater frequency. Thus, the only territories for which one can find recent data are Jamaica and Trinidad and Tobago. Even in the case of these two countries, large gaps exist in the documentation of unemployment. One has to be content with such fragments of information as can be found. Speculation is thus a major element in the contemporary analyses of the unemployment problem, and this paper is no exception.

An overall examination of available data for the Commonwealth Caribbean seems to indicate that little progress has been made with the unemployment issue over the last decade and a half. The Bahamas is the only English-speaking country in the Caribbean, which during the course of the 1960s reported near-full employment. However, unemployment has reappeared in The Bahamas over the past three years.

During certain periods, the rate of unemployment has remained unchanged, and the rate has become worse over other periods. Trinidad and Tobago is an example of the former. Its overall rate of unemployment has remained constant at around 14 percent of the labour force since the early 1960s. Jamaica and Barbados are representative of the latter. Jamaica's unemployment rate rose from 13 percent in 1960 to nearly 25 percent in 1972. The increase in Barbados was more modest, being 11 percent in 1960 and 13 percent in 1970. Comparable figures are not readily available for other territories in the area; but it is interesting to observe that the recent Economist Intelligence Unit Report on the Industrial Development of the Associated States posited an average of 20 percent unemployment rate for the islands in that group.

It is arguable that the rate of unemployment is somewhat exaggerated by the figures that have been just cited. In both Jamaica and Trinidad and Tobago, the major proportion of the unemployed labour force consists of female non-heads of households.

Unemployment for males is concentrated in the 15–24 age group. Thus one finds that in both countries, the rate of unemployment among male heads of households is around 9 percent. The view has been put forward that if one is concerned principally with bread-winners, the unemployment problem in the area is not as serious as the aggregate figures suggest.

This is nothing more than male chauvinism. One cannot sweep the problem of unemployment under the carpet simply because it is largely a female problem. One does not have to argue the point that females have as equal a stake in the economy as males. Beyond this, there are additional reasons why it will be unsafe to conclude that the overall figures overstate the magnitude of the problem. The principal reason is that no allowance has been made so far for under-employment. Here, the general evidence suggests that when under-employment – whether in terms of hours worked or income earned – is combined with open unemployment, all of the economies in the area are under-utilizing at least one-third of their labour force.

One cannot go much further with an empirical assessment of the problem. Apart from some limited information on occupational distribution and on levels of education, little else is known about the unemployed. One needs to get behind the bare statistics and build up detailed profiles of the social characteristics of this demographic. I will give a few examples of what is needed to ameliorate this problem.

Reference has already been made to the fact that young females account for a significant proportion of the unemployed. Statistically, this has expressed itself in an increase in female participation rates. But no one has yet investigated the reasons for this increase. Considerable analysis is therefore needed in this area, particularly on the question of work attitudes, which is consequential to the understanding of the new male entrants into the labour force. There is a general belief that males have a distaste for agricultural work and will leave a job in agriculture to migrate to the towns to join the ranks of the openly unemployed. This proposition is cited with such frequency that it comes as a surprise to many to find that there is not a single piece of empirical evidence available to support this thesis. The topic deserves, therefore, a place on the research agenda for the remainder of the 1970s.

In leaving the problem of measurement, the general observation can be made that a much more serious effort is required in assembling information on unemployment. If the policy towards unemployment is to be based upon anything more than shots in the dark, governments will need to allocate more resources to data collection. There is also a parallel need for greater involvement by all of the social sciences in studying the many dimensions of the question.

In searching for clues to our disappointing progress with unemployment, it will be instructive to briefly review the performance of our economies over the past decade or so. This is because the rate and pattern of output growth directly influence the demand for labour. An examination of growth rates in the GNP for the period 1960–1970 indicates that The Bahamas and St. Lucia were the only two territories to experience average annual rates of growth in excess of 6 percent, which was the target set by the United Nations for the Second Development Decade. On the whole, rates of growth in the large majority of territories were not much better than 4 percent, and since the rates of population growth was in the region of 2 percent to 2.5 percent, this left a mere margin for increases in per capita income.

Taking a longer view, one finds evidence of a slackening in growth rates in some countries. We have supporting evidence for this from estimates made by the OECD pertaining to the Growth of Real Product in Jamaica and Trinidad and Tobago. These figures reveal a slippage of growth rate in Jamaica from an average of 10 percent for most of the 1950s to one of 4 percent over the past decade. In Trinidad and Tobago's case, the situation was not much different. Starting with a historical rate of 8 percent, there was a slippage between 2 and 3 percent during the last few years of the 1960s.

Patterns of sectoral growth were not particularly helpful to the cause of employment. The data show that in most countries, mining or manufacturing were the leading sectors. The pattern of growth in both of these sectors has been typically labour-intensive such that increments to output have been more associated with increases in productivity than in employment. For example, in Jamaica where the mining sector grew fastest, its share in the GDP expanded by seven percentage points between 1960 and 1972. In Trinidad and Tobago, which grew faster than the other territories, its contribution to total employment rose only by one-fifth of a percentage of the manufacturing sector. In Trinidad and Tobago, the share of manufacturing in GDP expanded by six percentage points between 1960 and 1970, while employment in the sector increased by less than one percentage point.

In Caribbean economies in which mining or manufacturing were not principal contributors to growth, tourism tended to assume that role. This was especially the case in The Bahamas, where it was estimated that gross receipts from tourism expanded more than six-fold between 1963 and 1971. The evidence also suggests that tourism was the main engine of growth in Barbados and the Associated States.

Although tourism has tended to be more labour-intensive than mining or manufacturing, demand conditions in this sector are rather more volatile than in the other two sectors. Since 1970, the growth of tourism has tended to be less buoyant than in previous periods, leaving many territories with a problem of excess hotel capacity. Some territories have been even more badly hit, as the economy has virtually ground to a halt. Antigua is the classic case. Between 1963 and 1968, value added by hotels in Antigua increased at an average annual rate of 19 percent. The boom in this sector generated large increases in government revenue from import duties: imports nearly trebled in value over that period. The government was thereby encouraged to mount an ambitious loan programme to finance improvements to the infrastructure of the tourism industry (international airport, deep-water harbour, water). When growth slowed towards the end of the 1960s, the government found itself with a heavy debt burden. In 1971, it was estimated that the public debt (which was largely external) was equivalent to the total GDP and that the annual debt service amounted to approximately 75 percent of annual tax revenue.

Therefore, as far as employment-creation was concerned, the governments seemed to have placed their bets on the wrong horses. Particularly serious was the relative neglect of agriculture, which everywhere declined in relative terms, and in absolute terms in some places. Barbados and Trinidad and Tobago provide examples of the latter. In Barbados, on the basis of 1970 prices, value added by the agricultural sector declined from some $24 million in 1960 to around $17 million in 1971. Comparable figures for Trinidad and Tobago were $73 million and $65 million.

The problem in agriculture was that the export sector was sagging, and the rate of expansion of the domestic sector was insufficient to accommodate the rising local demand for food. With respect to export crops, sugar production showed a downward trend in every territory except Belize and Guyana. The same general trend was evident with regard to banana production in Jamaica and the Windward Islands and with minor crops such as cocoa, coffee and spices (except nutmeg). As far as domestic foodstuffs were concerned, some progress was registered in the production of poultry and pork, and vegetables, notably tomatoes. But altogether, import data make it clear that the gap between domestic demand and supply of food had widened. By 1971, the Commonwealth Caribbean was probably spending close to $200 million per annum on imported food. On the basis of rough data on direct and indirect employment coefficients, this sum was probably equivalent to the loss of over half a million jobs.

Another way of looking at the matter is to examine movements in the major components of demand in the economy. Here, two major variables come into play – the savings/investment relationship and the balance of payments. Regarding savings and investment, in the territories for which we have figures, there was a clear tendency for consumption expenditure to absorb a rising proportion of the GDP. For instance, in Jamaica consumption expenditure as a proportion of GDP rose between 1960 and 1971 from 83 percent to 87 percent, while the increase in Trinidad and Tobago was much more dramatic – from 66 percent to 81 percent. The consequential weakening of the savings effort meant that greater reliance had to be placed upon external sources for financing capital formation. Accordingly, in both countries, there was a marked increase in external financing as a proportion of the GDP. Taking the same years, the percentage figures for Jamaica were 2 percent and 19.4 percent, and for Trinidad and Tobago the percentage figures were 7.2 percent and 14.5 percent. Judged from the point of view of the domestic savings effort, the capacity for self-sustaining growth underwent a setback during the 1960s.

The end result of this pattern of financing was that the combined external public and private debt of the Commonwealth Caribbean is among the highest in the developing world. At the end of 1967, the total external debt of the area was estimated at nearly $3 billion, or some 93 percent of the GDP of the area. Of the $3 billion, about $2.5 billion represented the book value of foreign direct investment. This is probably an underestimated figure. Experience the world over shows that the market or replacement value could be as much as twice the book value. We should therefore be thinking in terms of a figure for direct investment that is close to $5 billion.

Apart from the question of foreign indebtedness, a large body of literature exists on the adverse effects of substantial foreign ownership and control on the rate of structural transformation and on the maximization of employment. This literature argues that whereas in the Caribbean, the major sectors of the economy are under foreign ownership and control, it is difficult to conceive of the country as being an economy in its own right. The principal decisions about resource allocation are taken by non-nationals, who are principally interested in maximizing their global profits after taxation. Accordingly, situations occur where corporate interest in the world is best served by maintaining enclave operations which have few linkages with the rest of the economy and which do not always produce at full capacity. Under these circumstances, foreign ownership operates against the interests of structural change and employment.

We do not need more than the tools of conventional economic analysis to show that it is highly debatable whether the Caribbean has secured substantial net benefits from the splurge of foreign investments which have occurred over the decade. Yet some economists continue to speak as though foreign investment is simply a resource gap problem, or a deficiency in savings. As Miss Watson and I have tried to show in the case of Trinidad and Tobago – if one starts off from a historical situation where the bulk of the capital stock is held by foreigners, in periods of rapid growth, the economy may find itself generating a sufficient surplus to finance its own investment, but still finds it necessary to borrow abroad. This has also been the Canadian experience. It is not enough to have a statistically adequate rate of domestic savings. This has to be backed by the capacity to take decisions about the disposition of these savings that accord with the national interest as opposed to private interests. It is at this point that the issue of ownership and control becomes particularly important.

Sir Arthur Lewis is among those economists who contribute our dependence on foreign capital to a lack of thrift on the part of the population, reflected in part by the failure to achieve a higher level of public saving in the government sector. With regard to the government sector, data for the past six years show that Jamaica has been the only Commonwealth Caribbean country to increase its surplus on current account relative to the growth of GDP. Elsewhere in the region, the rate of public saving tended to fall. In the case of some of the Associated States, it is more accurate to say that the rate of public dis-saving tended to increase. The Associated States have historically run budgetary deficits on current accounts covered by grants-in-aid from the United Kingdom.

Whether one agrees with Sir Arthur Lewis's analysis in its entirety or not, it is a matter of concern that fiscal discipline is lacking in certain parts of the Caribbean. On the revenue side, one finds a disproportionate share of direct taxes being contributed by wage and salary earners compared with companies and self-employed persons. In general, the entire tax structure tends only to be nationally progressive, since in the case of indirect taxes, the rates on luxury goods are much lower than would be suggested by their income elasticities. As far as expenditure is concerned, there is a pronounced tendency in some countries to readily commit actual or projected increases in revenue to consumption expenditure instead of to capital formation. Insofar as these increases in public consumption expenditure are devoted to wage and salary increases for public employees, this means that the budget tends to favour those in employment over the unemployed.

In relation to the balance of payments, the Commonwealth Caribbean countries have individually and collectively followed policies of restrain. As a result, the area has tended to accumulate reserves since 1960, notwithstanding temporary difficulties in Guyana in the mid-1960s, in Trinidad and Tobago in 1970 and in Jamaica in 1972. Despite this apparent soundness in the external position, the available data portray certain weaknesses in the balance of payments. One of these is the growing deficit in services, which became the largest single deficit item. Here, the main components of the deficit were freight and transportation, investment income and travel. Attention is just being given to the possibilities for curbing the growth in expenditure of foreign exchange on freight, by studying the feasibility of setting up a merchant marine. Sufficient thought has not yet been given to the growth of foreign travel. Imagine that the four independent countries in CARIFTA are spending over $40 million per annum on foreign travel! To summarize, during the last decade, we failed to serve the cause of employment on at least two counts. First, sufficient effort was not expended in the revitalization of agriculture and in the overall diversification of the economy. Secondly, the task of mobilizing local resources for job creation was not tackled thoroughly enough. Instead of increasing our rate of saving, we increased our dependence on foreign capital, thus continuing to reduce our control over the domestic surplus.

In view of these dismal results, what are the near-term prospects for employment?

First, we take a brief look at the supply of labour. As far as population growth is concerned, the United Nations has estimated that the population of the area will expand from 5 million in 1970 to around 6.4 million in 1985. The assumptions underlying these estimates are not known, but it is clearly crucial to assess possible trends in mortality, fertility and migration. G.W. Roberts had done this for Jamaica on the basis of the 1970 census data. He has shown that Jamaica can approach a situation of zero population growth by 1990 if a two-child family is achieved by 1985, and a net migration rate of 20,000 persons per annum is sustained throughout the 1970s and 1980s. On these rather optimistic assumptions, the potential labour force (i.e., the population in the age group 15–64) will expand by approximately 300,000 persons between 1970 and 1985. If a similar set of assumptions are made about the area as a whole, a rough calculation shows that we may need to create over one million additional jobs between now and 1985 if we are to absorb the increments to the labour force. When this is combined with the current backlog of the unemployed, it is clear that despite the best efforts at family planning and at maintaining migration outlets, we will still have a massive problem throughout the 1970s and 1980s. This calls for an investigation of traditional sources of growth. We can do no more than make a few brief points here.

With respect to agricultural exports, recent studies have shown that up to 1980, it is doubtful whether production and exports in the area will increase by as much as 2 percent per annum, with the exception of Guyana. It is believed in some quarters that there will be declines in production in the Leeward Islands, possibly in Barbados and perhaps in Jamaica. A similar view is taken of supply prospects regarding banana production in Jamaica and the Windward Islands. In any event, FAO projections indicate a high probability of a world surplus in banana production by 1980. World import demand is expected to reach 7.8 million tons by that year, while supply availabilities could well reach a level of as much as 13.7 million tons. In relation to citrus, annual rates of growth in world import demands are expected to level off at about 2 to 3 percent. And the prospects for most other agricultural products are not much better, at least as far as the Caribbean's major markets are concerned.

Altogether, the general evidence suggests that it would be imprudent to look for substantial increases in employment from the export agricultural sector. And it should be noted that just maintaining the present levels of exports requires the successful conclusion of an agreement with the Enlarged EEC on securing appropriate access terms.

Where the mineral sector is concerned, the outlook for output and exports looks brighter, but it is doubtful whether this will directly yield any large increments to employment. Regarding bauxite, the world demand for aluminium is expected to grow at an annual rate of 8 percent. If the Commonwealth Caribbean maintains its share of the world market, then considerable increases in output and exports can be expected. For instance, in planning to retain its share in the world market, Jamaica is gearing to boost its production of bauxite to 18 million tons by 1975 and 25 million tons by 1980. However, exports of bauxite itself will be stabilized to around 9 to 10 million tons since an increasing proportion of output will be processed into alumina.

The real impact of bauxite expansion will come when success is achieved with establishing facilities for smelting the bauxite into primary aluminium which can form the basis for more labour-intensive fabrication industries. Here, the principal obstacle is said to be the availability of cheap power. Here, several possibilities are being investigated. Jamaica is well advanced with negotiations for an oil refinery, which is expected to produce fuel oil for use in a thermal electric plant. Guyana is undertaking pre-investment work in the installation of a hydroelectric complex. Furthermore, consideration is being given to the utilization of Trinidad and Tobago's supplies of natural gas for smelting its ores. It is doubtful, however, whether any of these developments can increase employment before the mid-1980s.

A similar situation exists in regard to Trinidad and Tobago's petroleum industry. It is anticipated that the output of petroleum could nearly double by 1975 if it attains a level of 100 million barrels as compared with the 1970 level of 52 million barrels. In addition, it is hoped that a liquefied natural gas plant will come on stream in the latter part of the 1970s with a daily capacity of some 450 million cubic feet. Just as in the case of bauxite, employment should be greatly bolstered when the petrochemicals industry is developed to the stage at which forward linkages are established with final product industries. These developments may be as much as a decade and a half away.

Turning to tourism, the experience since 1970 has promoted more moderate forecasts of growth at least up to 1975. For example, it has been estimated that the percentage of U.S. tourists travelling to the Caribbean will drop from 61 percent in 1971 to 57 percent in 1975, whereas a 40 percent increase had actually been predicted for the Caribbean. Recent movements in the exchange rates of European currencies, in addition to inflation within Europe itself, may serve to narrow Europe's competitive edge over the Caribbean. But it should be recalled that the problems associated with the tourist industry are not solely those of price. Poor service and a narrow range of attractions are often cited among the limitations that affect the growth in tourist traffic, especially in repeat business.

More fundamentally, there is a point of view which questions whether Caribbean countries should allow uncontrolled growth of the tourist industry in its present form. Critics have been calling for a restructuring of the industry based upon small locally owned hotels and guest houses, which have strong backward linkages with other sectors of the economy, especially agriculture. Whether this re-organization of the industry will occur in time to affect employment during the remainder of the 1970s is a different question.

Given the limited prospects offered by the traditional export activities, attention should be paid to the scope for import substitution. As far as the large food bill is concerned, some steps are already being taken to reduce it through renewed efforts to step up location production. However, it can be argued that the measures taken so far are not sufficiently comprehensive. Most governments are proceeding upon the assumption that the achievement of self-sufficiency in food can be done largely through bringing idle lands into production. In Jamaica, it has become almost an axiom of policy to assert that the food requirements of the population can be met upon a few thousand acres of land. This position takes a most limited view of self-sufficiency, by using current levels of import expenditure as the measure of the deficit. If one were instead to set certain minimum targets for food consumption, particularly of proteins, with respect to the entire population, the land requirements would far exceed a few thousand acres of land. In other words, it is difficult to conceive of a comprehensive programme for feeding the population without significant land reform. This becomes even more essential when the land needs of potential agro-based industries are taken into account.

Another area in which present policies for agricultural development appear to be deficient concerns the restricting of demand. For instance, we shall not make sufficient progress with reducing the food import bill until we can find substitutes for imported cereals. Wheat flour is the most important item here. At the present time, cereals consume about one-third of the food import bill. Intensified efforts should be made to change the tastes of the population in favour of flours produced from local starches. Some experimental work is going on with respect to the mixing of wheat with bananas and yams to produce a local flour. If these experiments succeed, we should be ready to change our tastes accordingly. This is merely one example of the need for comprehensive consumer education programmes to encourage the population to develop a taste for local foods. In the Caribbean, even radical politicians publicly mourn when apples are placed on the negative list of imports.

A similar perspective is necessary for the development of new import substitution programmes for the manufacturing sector. Presently, we are importing about $900 million worth of manufactures annually, of which about $390 million consists of light manufactures. Compared to other developing regions and states, the Caribbean has not made much progress with import substitution. For example, we are still big importers of textiles, an item usually associated with the first phase of industrialization in other countries. Likewise, with intermediate and capital goods, we are behind with steel production and with the production of simple tools and machinery, such as the equipment used in the agricultural sector. It is only a slight exaggeration to say that we have not yet passed the hoe and machete stage.

Students of the subject have long recognized that a major obstacle to industrial development in the Caribbean is the proliferation of brands on the market, serving to fragment domestic demand, thus making it difficult to achieve the critical minimum size necessary for establishing production. Particularly dangerous is the tendency to confine local production to assembly operations, which means that the economy loses the benefits that could be derived from fully integrated operations. Motor cars are a case in point. Brewster and Thomas have made the viable case that if the Caribbean were prepared to accept a single make of car, we would be able to develop a fully integrated manufacturing process. However, we have so far concentrated on assembling several brands of knocked-down vehicles. The evidence suggests that these assembly operations involve a relatively small element of local value added, and tend to have a negative effect on the balance of payments. From the standpoint of employment and economic growth, it would clearly have been preferable to change the pattern of demand in favour of the integrated operation rather than accepting the demand pattern as given.

A final area for accelerated import substitution is services. Earlier in this talk, reference was made to the possibilities inherent in tourism. However, other areas such as freight and transportation warrant attention. At present, we load about 39 million tons of cargo in the Commonwealth Caribbean and unload about 28 million tons. These tonnages are larger than those in many countries which have a merchant marine. A grave problematic situation arises in that the major proportion of these cargoes consist of bulk items – bauxite, petroleum, sugar, bananas, all of which are under the control of multinational corporations. Yet, we cannot afford to despair over the matter since many countries have managed to successfully secure some of their bulk cargoes for their merchant fleet. Although the direct contribution of a merchant marine to employment may be small, the indirect and more long-term effects may be substantial if the establishment of the fleet facilitates the expansion of new exports.

To summarize this part of the analysis, the growth of employment over the remainder of the 1970s will principally rely on new efforts at import substitution where food, manufactures and services are concerned. If we also manage to perform the necessary groundwork during this decade, the next decade could see us emerge as important exporters of mineral-based manufactures. At minimum, progress in these two directions will require an appropriate macro-economic policy framework. Let us turn to discuss this question.

Much of the literature on macro-economic policy has been filled with discussion and debates on the appropriateness of devaluation and incomes policies as the principal instruments in a policy package for restructuring the economy. The advocacy of devaluation has been associated with the name of Sir Arthur Lewis. In a series of papers, he has argued that taking into account the paucity of natural resources and our tiny domestic markets, the long-term comparative advantage of the region lies in developing exports of labour-intensive manufactures. Accordingly, the main focus of policy should be on maintaining an internationally competitive level of wage costs. In a recent statement on the question of wage costs, Lewis claimed that "costs have become too high because our money incomes are determined for all economic activity by what the richest industries can afford to pay, namely the mines and the tourist industry without regard to the productivity level of other industries". "When one says of an economy that its money costs of production are too high in relation to the world prices for it to be able to provide full employment, this is the classic definition of an over-valued currency. Nearly all West Indian currencies are heavily over-valued. This is the basic reason for our high and steadily mounting unemployment." Thus, he has advocated a policy package, which emphasizes devaluation and an incomes policy.

The need for wage restraint has also been stressed by Dudley Seers. In his model of the open petroleum economy, Seers put forward the thesis that in an economy dominated by an enclave activity such as petroleum, the rate of growth in employment tends to be determined by four variables. These are the rate of growth in mineral exports, the rate of growth of productivity in the export sector, the tax rate and the import co-efficient. He argued that in such economies, for any given rate of growth in exports, the rate of growth in productivity in the export sector determined the change in employment in that sector and the reserve price of labour in the rest of the economy. Likewise, taxation was apart from labour income in the export sector, the main mechanism whereby indirect employment was created out of an expansion in enclave exports. In his view, an economy of this sort had a kind of wages fund, represented by the local payments of the enclave industry. Thus, an allowance of uncontrolled growth in wages corresponds with less employment.

The Seers strategy was less open than Lewis's strategy, as it introduced the import co-efficient, thus admitting the possibility of a more inward-looking strategy based principally upon import substitution. Nonetheless, the Seers model has been criticized. Like Lewis's model, it makes no allowance for the beneficial effects which a redistribution of income can have on both employment and growth. Furthermore, neither Lewis nor Seers took into account the effects of changes in the pattern of demand for domestically produced goods and services. Havelock Brewster has demonstrated that this latter variable has some explanatory significance in relation to the employment experience of Trinidad and Tobago, for example.

The World Bank has recently endorsed the Lewis strategy of devaluation and incomes restraint in its policy proposals for alleviating unemployment in Trinidad and Tobago. Since the World Bank suggests that the strategy is also appropriate for other CARIFTA countries, it will be useful to comment further on the strategy. Assuming that it is possible to implement a successful incomes policy, one can then ask whether a devaluation alone can produce the desired growth in employment. To begin with, the prices of nearly all of the major exports of the area are fixed in foreign currency, including sugar, bauxite, petroleum and bananas. The prices are also largely fixed for tourism since hotel rates are normally quoted in U.S. dollars. Thus, a devaluation will merely yield windfall profits to enterprises in these sectors without necessarily promoting direct expansion in employment. Indeed, since several of these industries are characterized by a high degree of foreign ownership, devaluation could hurt the balance of payments by leading to an increase in the outflow of investment income. The outcome would be to shift the distribution of the GDP in favour of non-nationals at the expense of nationals.

Furthermore, there is no certainty that a devaluation can produce an international cost advantage of sufficient size and permanence to favour the development of new exports or import substitution. Firstly, the import content of industry in the Caribbean is particularly high due to the region's reliance on imported materials, components and parts. Thus, the cost advantage will tend to be wholly a wage advantage to be sufficiently significant to justify new investment decisions. Apart from these supply considerations, no empirical analysis has been produced to show that high wage costs are the principal barrier to the expansion of new exports or to import substitution. As far as the possibilities cited earlier in this paper are concerned, such as the development of mineral-based exports and of import substitution in agriculture, it is apparent that the level of wage costs is not one of the main obstacles to these developments.

Under present conditions, it is wise not to be overly optimistic about the negotiation of a successful incomes policy. Given factors such as income inequality, foreign ownership and the political character of the trade unions, it is doubtful whether workers will readily accept a sustained cut in their real incomes. The same will be true for entrepreneurs as they primarily focus on short-term monetary gains.

All this is to say that a fresh start is needed. The desire to find a solution involving the use of the price mechanism is basic to all of the policy prescriptions offered thus far. It should be easily understood that in economies as fractured as those in the Commonwealth Caribbean, the reliance upon the price mechanism is in conflict with meaningful structural change. We will need to learn to operate an efficient disequilibrium system, which will involve the use of direct instruments of control over patterns of supply and demand. To search for a painless formula for change is to misunderstand the needs of change itself. Hard choices are required in the Caribbean if we are to provide a satisfactory stake in the economy for our less fortunate brothers and sisters.

Chapter 1.8

The Importance of Productivity Growth in the Caribbean

Address to the Caribbean Association of Industry and Commerce Annual Awards Banquet, At the Novotel Hotel, Gosier, Guadeloupe, May 26, 1989

Let me say how pleased I am to be here in this historic and charming city of Pointe-A-Pitre. Your meeting in this city symbolizes the historical imperative of bringing the English-speaking and French-speaking islands of the Caribbean closer together. We are at a moment when our common interests are becoming more apparent. We must dispassionately examine the scope for cooperation that undoubtedly exists and when we should meet to identify the crucially important elements in our common future.

No one is more knowledgeable about the question of Caribbean cooperation than Mr Clovis Beauregard. I had the good fortune of meeting him over 30 years ago when he was Executive Secretary to the Caribbean Commission, and I was then a mere student attempting to start my research. I still clearly remember the good advice that he gave me and his enthusiasm for bringing the Caribbean countries more closely together. We count ourselves fortunate to have in the Caribbean today men of the sagacity, experience and commitment of Mr Beauregard. I salute him.

The Importance of Productivity Growth

I now turn to the subject of my address, namely productivity growth. Productivity is a measure that encapsulates a number of critical elements: the quality of management, the skills and attitudes of the labour force, technological capability and the economic policy framework.

To unearth the requirements for productivity growth in the Caribbean, one first identifies the elements in the development situation and prospects to subsequently deduce the sources from which productivity growth has to emanate. This is how I propose to tackle the situation today.

The Development Situation

For over a decade or more, the large majority of Caribbean Community (CARICOM) countries have been experiencing slow growth, and in some cases, negative growth. Within the past two to three years, positive economic growth has been seen in some countries, but it is still too early to say whether this will be transitory or a continuing phenomenon.

The fundamental fact must be grasped that as very small countries, CARICOM countries should develop efficient tradeable production both in the form of exports and import substitutes. This point bears continued repetition since the tendency remains of drawing questionable distinctions between export growth and import substitution. It is not the case of either/or. Sustained growth requires both. Competitiveness has to be achieved in all sectors in the economy, not merely in terms of comparative levels of cost and prices but also in relation to picking the right products for output expansion from the point of view of demand and supply capability.

Science and Technology

The foundations of such a transformation lie in the establishment of adequate scientific and technological capability. Biotechnology can be an important tool in revolutionizing agricultural production, both in terms of higher yields per acre and greater uniformity in the size and quality of products. It will also facilitate more experimentation with new varieties of items, such as fruit, vegetables and fish, information technology and its companion, artificial intelligence systems, which are now being applied in virtually all sectors of economies. The textile industry, traditionally a labour-intensive activity, is now being computerized in the Federal Republic of Germany: in fact, about 60 percent of domestic textile production has been computerized. In Japan, where computerized applications are a predominant feature of the economy, it is expected that a fully robotized automobile plant will come into commercial production in 1993.

The Caribbean has little choice for survival and growth unless more determined efforts are made to quickly build up scientific and technological capabilities. Among other things, this necessitates a concentrated research and development effort. So far, research and development activities have been principally confined to universities and government agencies. The private sector should become more involved in research and development, making it a regular feature of their operations. At the University, we are planning, among other things, to establish science and technology enterprise parks, which would provide facilities for our staff to service the needs of the local business communities for research and development work and for business support services generally. We would be happy to collaborate with the private sector in such endeavours.

Tertiary Education

Research and development and greater scientific and technological capabilities need highly educated and trained people, particularly at the tertiary level. At the University, we have taken pride in the fact that over the 40 years of our existence, we have graduated some 35,000 students. However commendable that is, we have been merely scratching the surface. International statistics show that in all but one of the CARICOM countries, 5 percent or less of the population of university age is enrolled in a tertiary institution. This compares with double-digit figures for most of Latin America and Asia – usually in the range of 10 percent to 15 percent. The percentage in Europe – both west and east – is over 30 percent, and in North America the percentage is over 50 percent.

The situation is more striking for tertiary enrolment in science and technology. Singapore with a population of 2.6 million, compared to Jamaica with 2.4 million, has enrolled 18,000 students in comparison to 1,800 in Jamaica. The Caribbean faces a major knowledge gap at the tertiary level. A reduction in the knowledge gap would have many beneficial effects. It would improve the quality of teachers and curricula, thereby positively impacting the secondary and primary school systems. This is the essence of the University's thrust for fundraising: to expand and upgrade teaching and research to widen access to university education and improve its quality and relevance, with special reference to science, technology and management disciplines. For a start, we wish to make all of our students, irrespective of their discipline, computer literate.

Investment Requirements

If we are to achieve anything close to the directions that I have outlined, major public and private investments will be called for, both in the development of the knowledge base and its absorption by the productive sectors of the economy. For this to happen, there has to be substantial improvement in the overall economic environment for growth so that greater confidence and momentum is generated in the economy.

The Role of the Government

Governments have their role to play, partly in following sound macroeconomic policies that maintain credible exchange rates and price flexibility, sufficient to keep domestic costs and prices in line with those of major trading partners, while encouraging greater predictability and continuity in economic life.

The Private Sector

For the private sector, it has to develop a capacity of innovation – for trying new lines of production, and new markets, for working with governments to discourage capital flight and the continuance of black market and illegal trading. Private sector leadership has to motivate the entire workforce to deepen commitment to their jobs; to take pride in hard work, achievement and discipline which would reflect themselves in outstanding company performance, improved profitability and higher wages and salaries. The trade unions also have a motivating role to play in that connection. I have often wondered whether the time has not come to build productivity agreements within collective wage settlements, on a regular basis.

Concluding Remarks

Unless we can become high-productive, robust and competitive economies, we are likely to languish at the periphery of the world economy. The emergence of larger trading blocs – Europe after 1992, the Canada/US Free Trade Area, now reportedly being extended to include others, and possible developments in Japan and South East

Asia – indicate an important reality. If we are not prepared to seize opportunities, we will be left behind in the new wave of industrial and technological growth, just as we missed the boat in the golden decade of the 1960s.

I leave you with this message. We cannot lose time in working together to achieve our development goals. The University of the West Indies (UWI) is ready to do its part, and we look forward to collaborating with the private sector and with governments in meeting the challenges that lie ahead.

I thank you.

Chapter 1.9

The Knowledge Economy

Address in Honour of Dr Eric Williams, 2006

The subject of my lecture this evening is the Knowledge Economy and its role in the transformation and development of Caribbean countries. The title that I have chosen is a tribute to Dr Eric Williams in whose name this series of lectures was established.

Dr Williams was a man of many parts. What I would like to emphasize here is that he was an outstanding scholar and historian. Among the intellectual assets which he bequeathed was his work on *Capitalism and Slavery* that serves as a poignant reminder that the purpose of knowledge is to serve humanity. We should, in all our efforts to promote knowledge development, keep this objective before us.

The Knowledge Economy can be said to exist where continuing economic growth and development at rising rates are taking place based upon the increasing application of new or revised knowledge to economic activity covering the stages of investment, production, markets and trade. We are deemed to be in a knowledge society today because of the emergence of new computer-based products in world trade and the related growth of international trade in services representing over 50 percent of the value of total trade. Countries are mindful today that if they are to retain their share of the world market, whether in traditional categories such as food and beverages or new ones such as telecommunications, they have to step up the process of innovation and product development. They are obliged to become cost-competitive based on high and rising productivity, thereby becoming more attractive destinations for local and foreign investment, whether producing for domestic markets, or for export (outsourcing) or as sources of highly skilled migrants to join the workforce, hopefully on a temporary basis, in the developed countries.

The debate continues on whether these patterns of international specialization are consistent with balanced development in the world economy as a whole, and in the developing countries, in particular. In the limited time available this evening, I cannot significantly advance that discussion. In setting new rules for international trade in goods and services, such as in the Doha Round and similar endeavours being pursued at the plurilateral and bilateral levels, the Caribbean has to position itself to participate in these rising flows of trade in goods and services on terms advantageous to our development.

In turn, a major objective of our development policies should be to achieve and sustain high levels of international competitiveness based upon capacities to produce and export a wide range of goods and services to different destinations in the world. This represents a challenge to our capacity to produce highly educated people capable of running sophisticated operations based upon the latest technology. The highly educated will also be equipped to engage in scientific and investigative work that can yield improved and new products. They will be able to innovate at every stage of production and trade.

Much discussion has taken place at both national and regional levels on the transformation required to bring our educational systems in line with these requirements. The reforms which are more or less agreed among countries in the region include a major strengthening of the system of early childhood education. In this way, students can make a smooth transition to the primary levels and beyond; the need for improved and new schools, equipment, more highly trained teachers at all levels and improvements required in school nutrition programmes. At the primary and secondary stages, the task is also to produce a larger cadre of teachers in foundation subjects, principally English, mathematics and the sciences. We need to build up computer studies so that all students are able to attain computer literacy. At the secondary level, students should be afforded exposure to work-related activities in the technical and vocational areas so that a focus on employability can emerge as a major objective of that level of the system. It is indeed a major shortcoming commented on by institutions such as the World Bank, that only comparatively small proportions of the labour force in the region have had formal education in technical and vocational subjects.

In many ways, the tertiary level has to be the driver of the system. It should give students the opportunity to qualify in both professional and para-professional programmes, permitting students to enter the labour force at those levels; wherever feasible, it should provide for exposure to work experiences training in leadership strategies and increased knowledge in manufacturing processes. The tertiary system also needs to take the lead in promoting and conducting research and investigative work.

Merely to summarize the features of the different levels of the educational system is to illustrate the major gap between expected roles and present performance. Since I cannot go much further into every feature of the system, I shall concentrate on making additional remarks about the tertiary system and its future role.

Over the past two decades, it has become apparent that our tertiary system needed bolstering as it constituted a potential barrier to greater advancement of our development in the context of development needs and the opportunities to which I alluded earlier. The searchlight was then placed upon our low rates of access, especially to science and technology programmes. Without getting into elaborate detail, our access ratios were hardly at double digits. Comparable countries in Latin America, Asia and other parts of the developing world had access rates that at least doubled our own. A frequently cited example was Singapore, where with a similar population to Jamaica, there was more than twice the number of students enrolled at the tertiary level in science and related subjects.

A determined effort was then put in hand to step up the enrolment in Science, Technology, Engineering and Mathematics (STEM) subjects. Based on a substantial loan from the Inter-American Development Bank, the University of the West Indies (UWI) upgraded its laboratory and computer facilities to accommodate a larger intake, initiated strategies to augment and increase faculty in subjects where shortages were most acute. UWI has also provided financing to departments to invite visiting scholars in important specializations. Furthermore, the University has given allocations for research, including pilot research and development programmes. These initiatives have had a positive impact, but their sustainability has been endangered by continuing financial uncertainties and limited success in raising financial support from corporate and other donors, both within the region and further afield.

As far as access rates are concerned, St Augustine is the only campus that is currently enrolling more than half of its student population in science and technology. Cave Hill has made some advances in that regard, but at Mona, progress remains slow, largely because of the lack of qualified students to enter those faculties. At the same time, there continues to be rapid growth in social sciences and management courses. How to redress this persistent imbalance in the disciplinary distribution of the student population remains one of the most important challenges facing the University.

In the field of research, efforts continue to increase the flow of published work and to provide incentives to staff towards that end. Again, there are imbalances in performances among individual faculties, and according to those sources, difficulties persist with constraints such as high teaching loads and limited funding for research support, including collaboration with overseas scholars in areas of common interest. However, a positive development has been increasing in the number of endowed chairs that, among other things, require the holder to assume leadership in research in the particular field.

On a wider plane, UWI has been expected to lead in promoting the harmonious and efficient development of systems in technical and technological education in the region. There can be little doubt that given the paucity of the region's human and financial resources, the essentiality of achieving critical mass in establishing teaching in most of the disciplines involved, the limited opportunities available for developing highly trained faculty in the large majority of areas, all place constraints upon the supply of high-quality teaching. We also have the challenge of insufficient research studies, the stiff international competition for staff and securing appropriate international accreditation for programmes. It could be illusory to believe that the Caribbean can develop and sustain a large number of national tertiary institutions of the required quality.

It is possible to conceive of a situation where several national institutions in the region are networked to achieve critical mass, the required international accreditation and contribute towards the research effort. This was indeed the thinking behind the establishment of the Association of Caribbean Tertiary Institutions (ACTI), where it was envisaged that UWI, working on an equal basis with other tertiary institutions, would serve as a focal point for such a network. ACTI was expected to promote programme complementarity between institutions, each drawing upon its particular strengths to provide specialized training with arrangements for joint programme design and the development of distance courses. This would promote interaction between institutions, thereby facilitating student and faculty exchanges and collaboration in research.

One of the features of recent tertiary education has been the establishment of a comparatively large number of institutions, largely private ones, offering several degree and non-degree programmes. In certain respects, these developments are to be welcomed insofar as they increase access and, in some instances, offer lower-cost financing for students. In some instances, they also offer work-friendly programmes that are provided in the evenings and on weekends.

At the same time, an understandable anxiety exists on the extent to which overlapping and duplication are taking place, whether there has been sufficient 'Caribbeanization' of programmes and whether too much concentration has been placed on low-cost arts-based programmes that cover areas in which the region is already well provided, instead of the higher-cost science programmes.

Without in any way belittling the well-intentioned initiatives by private providers, a discussion is needed on making the system of tertiary education more closely attuned to the needs of the region.

Institutions should pay particularly close attention to market requirements rather than their particular educational ambitions. The criticism has been voiced that some initiatives are motivated more by the search for academic prestige without sufficient reference to staff capacities and the state of academic infrastructure by way of books, materials, computer and laboratory capacities and the needs of the market as expressed by current and prospective employers. The work of the University Council of Jamaica requires an endowment of greater resources to ensure that the process of accreditation of locally operating institutions takes adequate account of all of these factors.

I return to the subject of research and development. It is acknowledged that the region faces a major challenge regarding the expansion and upgrading of its research and development activities. The need for such improvements is a general feature of the new character of international trade. Because of the intense competition now prevailing, countries need to pay particular attention to quality control and to the enhancement of the peculiar features of their products and the brands associated with them. This is most apparent in trade in processed foods such as fruit juices, nectars, jams, soups and processed meats. The current situation is an outcome of the considerable and complex regulations originating in the desire of developed countries to achieve certain objectives in areas such as food safety and security. The region has already implemented many initiatives in this area. Some of them are beginning to bear fruit.

Another area of great relevance to this discussion is the service sector. Apart from established industries such as tourism, which needs greater attention, the region is also exhibiting strengths in fields such as entertainment (music, theatre, film), fashion design and sports, among other areas. Increased vigilance is needed to protect copyright and related techniques for safeguarding product brands; this is a field in which awareness is building. Hopefully, governments acting together will work assiduously to advance our competitive strengths through greater support for research and development involving product development and innovation.

I think I have said enough to indicate that a huge task awaits our governments, private sectors and people, as we endeavour to ascend the steep and slippery slopes of international competition. In the field of international trade, the region has contended successfully with many challenges. I have no doubt that we shall rise to those now currently before us.

Section 2

The Role of the University in the
Development Process

Introduction to Section 2

The twelve papers in section 2 of these collected papers discuss the University of the West Indies as an agent of Caribbean economic and social development through its leadership role in human resource development and in knowledge creation and dissemination at the tertiary level. The papers also explore the University's contribution to Caribbean economic integration policies and strategies, its involvement in community and public outreach and its activities that assist in strengthening links between the Caribbean and the wider world. Each of these subjects is covered in varying detail in the papers, some of which also address the changes required in the University to ensure continued relevance to help resolve Caribbean development challenges.

The papers are perhaps better appreciated if the reader starts with the address entitled "National Development: Aspects of the Task Ahead", given in September 1980. In this paper, McIntyre presents his wide-ranging analytical perspectives on the elusiveness of economic development, the liberating influence of constitutional independence on national governments that find themselves faced with "the challenge of generating economic development within a framework of social justice". He also discusses the experiment in popular participation in decision-making, authoritarian tendencies, elevated bureaucratic control and political patronage in public policies for social justice in societies with weak structures for social accountability. He argues for a more expanded role for individual initiative, effort, discipline, thrift and achievement within a framework of social responsibility. This will enable us to attain "a new infusion of community initiative in crucial areas of national life", which again underscores the critical importance of the human factor in economic development. The paper also touches on more traditional macro-economic issues and Caribbean integration.

The role of the UWI as a promoter and facilitator of economic development is introduced in the Eric Williams Memorial Lecture entitled "The West Indian University Revisited". There the reader finds a statement of the University's role in laying the foundations for the transition from resource-led development to knowledge-led development. After giving a succinct account of the UWI's record in teaching, research and outreach, McIntyre outlines the development imperatives for the Caribbean with a focus on the requisite knowledge base. The University is positioned to contribute to the growth of more sophisticated human resources, to expand the research and development effort, to elucidate the concept of a Caribbean identity and to provide information and expertise on regional and global affairs.

The paper "Confronting the Challenges of Change" interprets the role of the UWI as a change agent preparing future Caribbean leaders, improving social cohesion and building science and technology capacity in a situation of under-supply of tertiary-educated human resources. McIntyre identifies changes required at the UWI, including re-orientation of the curriculum towards science and technology and social sciences, distance education, funding for economically disadvantaged students with academic potential, and improvements in operational efficiency. He advocates for greater efforts to be made to network with regional and extra-regional universities and higher education institutions for academic programme delivery and research. He explains the need for capital mobilization from local, regional and international donors. These issues are also addressed in his papers entitled "Opening Our Windows to the World", "Annual Address to the University Community in 1993" and "Vice Chancellor's Roundtable Address" in 1995 that provide updates on major developments at the University.

"Challenges Facing UWI for the 21st Century" is a fuller statement of the economic development challenge, discussing the requirements in terms of human resource development and the needed changes at the UWI to make the institution more effective and impactful. The paper stresses that knowledge should be "the central ingredient for economic growth and development", necessary for the modernization of traditional economic sectors and the development of new ones. Science and technology, multi-disciplinary and inter-disciplinary approaches, and a global outlook should be reflected in the objectives and modus operandi of the University. McIntyre states: "overall, UWI has to promote itself as a centre for innovation. ... The centre of dynamism for the region stretching into different parts of the world." For McIntyre, a 21st -century UWI would have a much larger enrolment of both on-campus and off-campus students, be engaged in mixed mode teaching, have substantial graduate education and research programmes and have a dynamic research agenda that responds to Caribbean knowledge needs as well as being internationally competitive. The University should also be engaged in more international collaboration, be more efficient and more financially independent of government subventions.

After a hiatus of nine years, McIntyre returned in 2002 to the topic of the role of UWI in Caribbean development. His presentation in 2002 entitled "Address on the Occasion of the Opening of the Alister McIntyre Building, Cave Hill Campus, October 2009" and "Address – Speaking Notes" at the UWI Mona Campus in Jamaica is the first of his subsequent attempts to draw attention to fundamental changes in the global environment and their implications for the Caribbean and its principal institution of higher education and research. The paper reminds readers of the primary role of the UWI over its forty years of existence, namely, to prepare leadership for constitutional independence and establish a Caribbean scholarship and reputation for high-quality teaching and research. He also argues for the desirability of a shift to a more internationalist character and agenda, thus not abandoning but instead consolidating its original mission. This shift is seen as particularly warranted in recognition of the globalization of educational services and accompanying changes in world trade systems.

"Striving for Excellence" elaborates on the new global agenda and renders a particular emphasis on globalization, poverty eradication, crime, international migration, and emergent medical and health problems such as HIV/AIDS. The success in building relevant human resource capacity would entail the adoption of cross-disciplinary and multi-disciplinary approaches, knowledge of the languages of neighbouring countries and emergent economic powers, and generally situating the UWI as a "window to the outside world".

Two of his papers focus on the role of the UWI in advancing Caribbean economic integration. "Notes on Governance and Decentralization in the Context of the Regional University" sets out why the UWI is viewed by Caribbean governments as a regional institution, while his "Address on the Occasion of the Opening of the Alister McIntyre Building, Cave Hill Campus, October 2009" and "Address – Speaking Notes – Opening of the Alister McIntyre Building, University of the West Indies, Mona, September 2, 2002" outlines the instrumentality of the UWI's intellectual efforts in promoting and fostering Caribbean integration from the conception of regional free trade into its evolution to the CARICOM Single Market and Economy.

"Productivity and Efficiency Issues in UWI: Some Working Notes", written in 2005, is a discussion on the internal efficiency considerations for the regional university, including the fuller utilization of the teaching and research capacity of the institution and its unit cost of operation.

Chapter 2.1

Confronting the Challenges of Change

Vice Chancellor's Address to the University Community Academic Year, 1991

Members of the University community, colleagues, friends, it is my pleasure to open the doors to the start of another Academic Year and to welcome you all at this time.

I know some of you may be facing the year with some amount of trepidation, based on your experience of last year's introduction of the Semester System. But I can assure you that we have been giving a great deal of attention to finding solutions to make the change less disruptive.

This year we expect you to find better systems in place and staff better oriented and able to advise students. Any major change such as we have made in shifting to the Semester System will have its share of teething troubles. But once the new systems have moved smoothly into gear, both students and staff will begin to reap many benefits.

The administration has spent these past several months of the summer reflecting on the mission of the University, reviewing progress and planning our strategies to strengthen our institution.

We are now poised to move forward with even greater confidence, mindful of the sense of purpose, the drive and the commitment which we shall all have to display if we are to achieve our goals.

The times ahead are challenging ones. The reality of economic hardships throughout the region is no secret. Indeed, our policymakers have repeatedly warned us that the challenges facing us in the immediate future are difficult to resolve.

However, I maintain that as an institution of higher learning, we cannot afford the indulgence of negative thinking. I think here of the well-known adage that the Chinese word for crisis is composed of two characters, one representing danger and the other representing opportunity. Our job, colleagues and friends, is to focus on opportunity, and to bear in mind the old Senegalese proverb that the opportunity that God sends does not wake those who are sleeping.

Let us ask ourselves what kind of university should be in place to serve the region's present and future needs.

It is clear to me that our challenge is to work ceaselessly to find means of turning our situation around to help create the conditions where meaningful development will be more than an empty aspiration for the people of the region.

From my own perspective as an economist, I believe that future growth in the region will greatly depend upon whether or not we can successfully make the transition from our present pattern of development, which is largely based on the utilization of natural resources, to one reliant upon human resources and knowledge as the principal ingredients. Therein lies the challenge for all of us. That challenge is to prepare the men and women who enter this institution for leading the region. With respect to both staff and students, their membership of the University community comes with the responsibility to assume that leadership, and we should never miss an opportunity to remind ourselves of this obligation.

In preparation for this leadership role, staff and students should adopt better work attitudes and habits. I ask each of you in your interaction with students and among yourselves to recognize that the mere possession of a university degree is not an ultimate destination. People who graduate from or work with this institution should be cognizant that it is more important to be educated than to show that you are educated. Thomas Huxley's reminder that the great purpose of life is not knowledge, but action should not be lost on any of us, irrespective of our position at the University.

I put this challenge before you because we always need to bear in mind the primary purpose of this University. It is to build the future of the West Indies, to build the future on a base of educated West Indian people who are fully prepared to work relentlessly for the betterment of the region.

As should be expected of the management of any organization, from time to time, we pause to examine how well we are achieving the objectives for which we were established. You will be interested to hear that recently, we conducted a series of on-the-demand studies for tertiary graduates, and the results were simply a confirmation of what we knew already. At present, the higher education system in the region is failing to turn out a sufficient number of trained persons to meet the demand existing in our countries. As a result, the entire region is experiencing serious shortages of high-level manpower. By way of illustration, we have estimated that over the period 1991 to 1996, the annual demand for all tertiary students by the region's private sector will be between 4,800 and 7,200.

I invite you to compare this demand with the University's annual capacity output. Currently, we are issuing about 2,600 degrees, diplomas and certificates. Other tertiary institutions in the region are cumulatively awarding about 1,400 certificates and diplomas.

When you add the total output of University of the West Indies (UWI) and those other institutions, the figure is 4,000 persons emerging each year from these institutions. On the whole, therefore, there is a significant gap between supply and demand. At the same time, we should not forget that each year the region loses about 1,500 highly skilled professionals.

I ask you to bear in mind that these estimates which I have quoted related only to the private sector. If one were to add public sector demand, one would find that we are in fact facing acute manpower shortages at professional and decision-making levels throughout the entire Caribbean region. So much for demand – but what about supply? My strong belief is that if the University fails to respond quickly to this urgent need for more highly trained manpower, the region will continue on the well-trodden path of importing high-cost management. While we welcome access to those skills, we have to be aware that in some cases, such persons have been educated by their countries to meet their specific demands, and therefore may not have been adequately prepared to adapt and amend their expertise to be in alignment with our specific socio-economic requirements.

In examining manpower needs, we have pinpointed specific shortages in certain areas. These include engineering, computer science, education, biological sciences and management.

It gives me a great deal of satisfaction to note that one of the most positive outcomes of the recent Caribbean Heads of Government Conference was an initiative to promote a scheme for the free movement of skilled professionals within the region. Once the scheme is in place, UWI graduates will be able to work in any English-speaking Caribbean territories without work permits.

I am inclined to believe that the significance of this development has not been sufficiently appreciated. I would have expected more commentary in our regional media on the implications of this important development.

I had spoken about the emigration of professionals from the region. I do not believe that the majority of those people who migrate from the region do so because they have no love for their countries or no great hopes for their future here. Rather, I strongly feel that they leave for lack of opportunity to extend themselves fully, to continue to hone their skills and to be adequately compensated. This seems to be something of a paradox. While our best people leave to be welcomed by developed countries and to be given accolades and rewards that they deserve, we continue to import skills. Now, with this bold and forward-thinking move, our governments have made an effort to reverse that trend, and I heartily commend them.

The Caribbean Association of Industry and Commerce (CAIC) and the West Indies Commission also deserve our commendations for actively promoting this initiative.

The efforts of the CAIC and the West Indies Commission reflect an understanding that the world around us is changing at a remarkably rapid pace. We should now make haste to embrace the forces of change for the sake of our people's development and the continued growth of our countries. We are forced to embrace change – we have no choice. My senior colleagues and I are convinced that the University must become one of the leading institutions in responding to and influencing the process of change. In that context, we need to develop a much stronger network of links with the international academic community. We should increasingly serve as a window to the outside world, a window which will allow into our midst those new and existing developments that are taking place in the wider world, a window through which we may share some of our unique knowledge, skills and facilities, and the research capabilities which members of our own community have successfully developed.

With this in mind, we shall be giving particular attention to two main areas this year. First, we are presently in discussion with a number of universities in the United Kingdom and North America with a view to establishing a series of exchange programmes that will be open to both staff and students. Secondly, we are taking a careful look at the extent to which we utilize our facilities and are identifying possibilities for using our classrooms and facilities during the long summer months. Accordingly, we shall be giving priority attention to the development of Summer School programmes. Such programmes can be an important vehicle for increasing access to the University for people in both the region and outside.

In addition to examining our relationship with the wider world, we have been taking a close look at relationships between the University and the several communities with which we interact directly on a daily basis. We are constantly reminding ourselves that a university is a living organism that draws its sustenance from the society it serves.

Universities in developing countries, in particular, must work hard to foster strong links with their communities. We can do this by finding means of improving social cohesion. We can do this by increasing our capacity for the productive application of science and technology. We can do this by identifying the means through which the Caribbean people can understand each other better.

We are not unmindful of the awesome responsibility which is ours. The results of our efforts at planning and developing strategies will demonstrate this recognition. As you already know, prominent among the several initiatives which we have taken in recent months to strengthen the University is the preparation of a Development Plan that takes us to the year 2000. The plan is wide-ranging and seeks to build upon the capabilities of every campus, faculty and department.

Based on our renewed commitment to developing the human potential of the region, we are aiming for a 50 percent increase in enrolment by the end of the decade. That is, we plan to move from 12,000 students to 18,000 students. While not unmindful of the importance of the humanities in providing a well-rounded education, we shall be placing major emphasis on science, technology and management studies. Our drive to increase enrolments will also encompass the non-campus territories. Here, we hope to use the facilities of our distance teaching network and our continuing education programmes to achieve an above-average increase in the number of students.

The increased numbers will doubtless make major demands on the University's infrastructure; hence, we have been taking a candid look at our levels of efficiency, particularly in the area of administrative services. We have completed management audits of the Bursary, Registry and Maintenance Services. These have pinpointed several areas where we can improve our operational effectiveness, and we are now turning our attention to the implementation of those recommendations.

The drive for efficiency extends to our use of resources for teaching and research. We shall shortly begin a programme of work to improve our cost-effectiveness in these fields. This will include projects of programme budgeting and zero-based budgeting.

These efforts to improve efficiency proceed alongside the initiatives which we have been taking to improve the salaries and conditions of work of our academic staff. The outcomes of the WIGUT negotiations on all three campuses have been a cause of satisfaction. You have my assurance that this is an ongoing area of concern to all categories of staff. My message to you all is that we owe it to ourselves and the people we serve to make sure that while we look forward to and enjoy better salaries and working conditions, we should also do our utmost to deliver better service.

I will now turn to some of our activities and initiatives in the academic sphere to prepare the University to meet the challenge of change management.

We are working towards concluding arrangements with the Cultural Training Centre to introduce a degree programme in the creative arts. On the Mona Campus, we are starting a television service which will be a major step forward in the training of students in mass communication. This service is expected to come on stream in the course of the Academic Year. Recently, we went on the airwaves with Radio Mona, an initiative which has received favourable comments from the University community and persons within the reach of the radio signals.

On the St Augustine Campus, many activities are gaining increased momentum, including the continuing education programme in agricultural technology. The same is true at Cave Hill, where advances have been made in areas such as the marine sciences.

In the non-campus territories, on the basis of funds we have received from Canadian International Development Agency (CIDA), we expect to establish UWIDITE stations in those countries that do not now have them. We shall also be enlarging and improving the range and quality of courses everywhere, including at stations such as Montego Bay, where we hope to finalize the establishment of a UWIDITE station to serve western Jamaica.

I also want to mention that we have been examining the matter of tuition fees. A group of experts has prepared a report on the more economic structure of student fees. We intend to subject this report to rigorous analysis within the University in the context of the difficult financial situation in the region and the possibility of some parents and students being able to pay for at least part of their education.

The flip side of the coin is that we have been working diligently to get more scholarships and bursaries for needy students. We have had one recent donation of over J$1m for an emergency loan fund on the Mona Campus, and we are turning our energies to seeking similar facilities for the Cave Hill and St Augustine campuses.

We know that many of our bright young people fail to take advantage of a university education because they cannot afford it. Financial assistance for students will therefore become an even more urgent imperative in the immediate period ahead when our economies and their financial capacity will probably grow at only modest rates. If you bear in mind our resolve to increase the output of graduates, the need for us to secure more scholarships and grants from private sources becomes most apparent.

I want to share with you some developments concerning the Association of Caribbean Tertiary Level Institutes which is more commonly known as ACTI. You will be pleased to know that it is now in place. Its establishment has significant implications for education in the Caribbean. This body comprises the heads of all tertiary level institutions in the Caribbean – teacher training colleges, the College of Arts, Science and Technology in Jamaica – technical training colleges and so on.

There are several excellent reasons for the existence of ACTI. In the first place, we shall be able to achieve greater cooperation among these institutions. Another important rationale for ACTI is better integration of their programmes with those of the University. In addition, ACTI will facilitate accreditation arrangements so that people can move more easily from institutions such as teacher training colleges into university programmes. One final point is worth bearing in mind. We shall, for the first time, be able to sit together to develop joint programmes and curricula.

ACTI is expected to play an integral role, for it presents us with a means of pooling our resources at the tertiary level.

I am privileged to have been elected as the first President of ACTI, and our 1991 assembly is scheduled to take place in Antigua in November. Already committees have been set up to begin work on such matters as accreditation and programme development.

All of these activities and initiatives referred to might not have had such a good chance of succeeding if we did not have the support of a number of institutions, friends of the University, the private sector and the governments of the region.

Last year, the Canadian Government provided us with a grant of CAN$10 million to support our work in human resources development, sustainable development and institutional strengthening. Our programmes with the European Communities continue, and our project with USAID Management Education has moved into its second phase.

The Government of Germany has provided a further J$13 million for the Fertility Management project under the direction of Professor the Hon. Hugh Wynter and the Government of Japan has donated an electron microscope to the Mona Campus.

Several foundations continue to support projects across campuses and faculties. Just yesterday, I received word that the Ford Foundation has approved a grant of US$1 million for the development of the Social Sciences. I am pleased to tell you that the Development and Endowment Fund is getting into stride across the region. This fund is indicative of the tremendous support we have received from the private sector and our alumni.

I single out the work of the Appeals Committees, which are moving ahead in many of our contributing territories and abroad. I think especially of the Jamaica Committee under the chairmanship of the Hon. Dennis Lalor, which has received pledges in excess of J$25 million from members of the Century Club, each of which has donated J$1 million or more.

We are also pleased with the progress made in Trinidad and Tobago, in Barbados and in some of the Organisation of Eastern Caribbean States (OECS) countries.

I think that is evidence of the recognition which our institution has among the people of the region, as well as among the international agencies and overseas governments that continue to support us.

The credit goes to the people who make up the University community. This includes professors, lecturers, administrators, the support staff and those students who continue to demonstrate the excellence, which is part of the West Indian heritage.

I am convinced that the governments of the region are doing as much as they can to fund the University. While many will argue that public resources should be concentrated on improving primary education, we should bear in mind that it is the tertiary system that will provide more highly trained teachers to achieve the desired results at the primary level. Hence, as the state of the economies of our various countries continues to limit the availability of public funds, careful attention should be paid to ensuring that allocations for tertiary education are commensurate with the tasks assigned to that part of the education system.

Finally, I appeal to the people of the Caribbean to recognize that in the UWI, we have a key that can unlock the West Indian potential for economic and cultural growth.

I appeal to you to nurture, support and encourage our University as it works to unlock our great potential.

In return, we promise a renewed commitment to excellence and to the prudent use of resources. We reaffirm our dedication to the task of helping the region to deal successfully and confidently with the challenges of change.

May I close by wishing you all a successful and productive Academic Year.

Chapter 2.2

Opening Our Windows to the World

Vice Chancellor's Address to the University Community, Academic Year – 1992–1993, September 24, 1992

Excellencies, members of the diplomatic corps, friends, members of the community of the University of the West Indies, once again, I take great pleasure in addressing you at the start of the Academic Year.

Today, I would like to revert to some of the themes that I have been emphasizing in addresses both within and outside of the University. I do so because of my strong conviction that we have to be extremely alert and sensitive to the rapidly changing environment in which we have to survive and grow. I shall be a bit long this afternoon, but I crave your indulgence.

I start with the observation that we are on the threshold of what I believe can be a period of unprecedented growth for the University. This path of growth in which we are entering is in response to the various development initiatives which we and others are taking to accelerate the pace of economic and social progress in the region. Caribbean countries are now working to ensure that they are not left out of the picture in the face of the sweeping social and political changes taking place all over the world. The report of the West Indian Commission draws attention to the fact that these developments will impinge upon the economic prospects of the region and its external economic relations.

As I have mentioned on several occasions, we are witnessing the emergence of a multi-polar world economics of new leaders in trade and finance and shifts in patterns of production and trade that are increasingly favouring knowledge-intensive products. It is also worth emphasizing again that new patterns of regionalization are unfolding in the world economy. As everyone knows, the European Community has moved towards establishing a Single Market, the USA, Canada and Mexico have recently completed the negotiation of a North American Free Trade Area in which our place remains to be determined. A variety of economic and cooperation arrangements are being worked out in Latin America. We have to assess how best we can relate to these developments.

Closer to home, Venezuela and the Dominican Republic have applied for membership in Caribbean Community (CARICOM). A road is being constructed to link Guyana and Brazil, and Guatemala's recognition of Belize opens new opportunities for cooperation between CARICOM and Central America. The French Antilles, the Netherlands Antilles and Surinam are all looking for new pathways for cooperation with us. The remaining non-English-speaking countries of the eastern Caribbean are also particularly interested in strengthening their links with CARICOM countries and institutions. What do these changes mean to us in our island home, in Belize, in

Guyana? I quote from the West Indian Commission: "These events bring home to us with vivid immediacy how fast things are moving and how easily small players in the game can be cast aside or overwhelmed by events that have nothing to do with them. As a result, West Indians feel they deserve to be offered much more and sense that they are in danger of receiving much less in a dangerous world."

At the same time, we are battling on the domestic front many more threats than ever before in our recent history. The old enemies are active: unemployment, deficient social services, poverty, crime, juvenile delinquency and powerful new ones are with us: the evil trade in drugs, growing indiscipline, disadvantaged women and homeless children, the spread of a culture of corruption. Together, we must confront these problems. Together, we must work relentlessly and urgently to expand the opportunities for human development in our own sphere of activity. This translates into a redoubling of efforts to increase access to University education, to upgrade the quality of University education and to strengthen its impact on the other levels of the education system.

On a more general plane, whether in relation to our external relations or the domestic problems of underdevelopment, the University has to lead the way in helping the region to fashion strategies, approaches and actions to address these problems. We have to provide the intellectual leadership, working our way through the conceptual clarification of issues to the development of practical problem-solving approaches. We have to provide a focal point for networking and collaboration at the institutional level with overseas countries. However, this in no way diminishes our primary task. That is to provide increasing numbers of graduates who enlarge the technical and managerial capabilities of our countries to achieve greater international competitiveness and reap the fruits of global developments that are taking place. As I have said before, the proximate task of the University in human resources development has to be set against the present and prospective shortfalls in the supply to highly educated and trained people. I have mentioned many times that the results of recent studies show that over the period 1991–1996, the private sector in the region will require somewhere between 4,800 and 7,200 tertiary level graduates per annum. As you all know, at the present time, UWI produces about 2,600 graduates per year, the rest of the tertiary system about 1,400 per year, while the net migration of tertiary trained people is about 1,600 persons. Accordingly, net current output is only about one-half to one-third of private sector needs. When the requirements of the public sector are added, it is clear that the region faces major shortfalls in the supply of high-level personnel in the period ahead.

Those of you who are familiar with the UWI's Ten Year Development Plan will know that we plan to increase our enrolment by 50% over the decade of the 1990s. The role of off-campus programmes will be critical in achieving these targets. The physical plant at the three campuses will not be able to support such a growth in enrolment along conventional lines. More importantly, we know that for many people, it is not easy to leave jobs and families to go to Barbados, or Trinidad and Tobago, or Jamaica for the time that it takes to get a certificate, diploma or degree. Our response is to build up the delivery capability of our distance teaching programme and cement our linkages with other tertiary institutions which offer associate degree and certificate programmes. That would reduce the length of time students will be required to spend on one of our three campuses.

I have previously drawn attention to the critical role which ACTI – the Association of Caribbean Tertiary Institutions – has to play in these developments. For those of you who may not be aware of the work of this institution, of which I am privileged to be president, it is designed to encourage greater cooperation between the tertiary institutions in the region as well as the better articulation of their programmes with those of the University. I repeat that there is a great necessity for more inter-institution collaboration and cooperation in education if the region is going to make the best use of available human and financial resources for the benefit of individual countries and the region as a whole. ACTI is presently focusing its attention on developing a scheme of associate degrees that will offer an alternative for University entry and wherever possible, advanced standing for transfer into degree courses.

I am most encouraged by the increasing recognition being shown by colleagues that we cannot stand aloof from these developments. We should roll up our shirt sleeves and join the tertiary institutions on an equal footing in a combined effort to strengthen their capabilities to deliver University level courses and to work out complementary courses among themselves and with the universities. In this latter context, I am also gratified to observe the active role which the University of Guyana (UG) is playing in ACTI. This enlarges the areas in which we can build our collaboration with UG. Speaking personally, I look forward to the day when UWI and UG will both be part of the University system for the English-speaking Caribbean. Undoubtedly there are difficulties in the way of achieving this goal, and we should tackle them in a timely manner and with a sense of purpose and resolution.

In a wider context, we need to sharpen our perception that UWI is part of a wider world. In the age of interdependence in which we now live, all countries have to face the reality that we are becoming increasingly linked with other countries in the world through the globalization of production, trade and finance. Furthermore, in the social field, problems such as drug trafficking, communicable diseases, refugees and environmental degradation are increasing without respect for national boundaries. We cannot stand aside from these developments in the false hope that we can remain islands unto ourselves. Universities as centres of enlightenment and understanding have to fashion responses to the new requirements of the age and point the way forward for the societies that they serve. UWI has to be part of this general trend. In our own case, we need to move beyond the task presented to us in the 1960s which was that of "Caribbeanizing" UWI. I believe that we responded well to that challenge. Today, in all of our faculties, we have programmes with a strong Caribbean content, under Caribbean leadership and responding to local and regional needs.

Now, as we move towards the end of the century and into a new one, our task is somewhat different. While we continue to stress local and regional relevance in our work, we have in addition to prepare our people to function successfully in a global academic environment. We have to build a greater capacity to keep abreast of what is going on in the wider world. We have to strive even harder than we have done so far, to innovate, wherever possible, to lead and to find niches in the wider world for our intellectual and technical involvement. We have, in effect, to become much more outward-looking in our thinking. This will inevitably make greater demands on us as an academic community, but the opportunities presented by this era of interdependence open up breathtaking possibilities for institutional and personal growth. If we fail to seize them, if we fail to comprehend that the future requires the best and not just the passable, if we delude ourselves into believing that we can accommodate mediocrity and low productivity under the guise of an outmoded nationalism or regionalism, we will increasingly become an ignored or past relic of a forgotten era.

Several countries in the Third World are now battling against the erosion of their University systems which has occurred over the past decade and a half. In several instances, this has been the outcome of shrinking resources and academic neglect. The process of reconstruction is proving to be both difficult and costly. Many institutions are openly questioning whether they can return to the academic levels which they once enjoyed and how they can cope with the stringent requirements of the new age. Some are virtually at the point of despair. Fortunately, the UWI has shown greater resilience over the years, thanks to the sustained efforts of staff and students as well as those of contributing governments and supporters. But this provides no ground for complacency. We cannot afford to stand still. We have to work unceasingly to push ahead and to make our presence felt in intellectual terms.

In thinking about the position of our institution and of the region as a whole in the emerging global scenario, the University should endeavour to contribute to the serious intellectual enquiry now underway concerning the relationships between concepts such as globalization, interdependence, a single superpower system, a new world order and people empowerment. In some situations, many of these ideas are reconcilable. Others are not. For example, in the field of production, globalization could involve either greater centralization or decentralization in decision-making dependent upon whether changing patterns of specialization and competitiveness are associated with shifts in the loci of decision-making. A single superpower system implies greater centralization unless it is accompanied by a strengthened multilateral system of global governance. Likewise, people empowerment need not mean less central government; it could mean a more effective central government with greater legitimacy and authority.

We need to re-think the ideas of the nation state and the region in this changing conceptual context. Undoubtedly, there are strong forces of a socio-cultural nature calling for reaffirmation and consolidation of our identity as peoples. How to reconcile this with the propulsive forces of technological change that are driving us in a different direction represents one of the major intellectual challenges of our time. The University is obligated to assume its leading role in this task of intellectual clarification and innovation, starting first with how our own institution should respond to these apparently divergent trends.

As part of that response, we should increasingly dispense with parochial notions about department, faculty and campus. We ought to consciously promote greater linkage and collaboration at all of those levels, making sure that we take the fullest possible advantage of our regional structure. I call upon everyone in the University to give the fullest possible attention to the advantages of our regional status. Without so doing, we run the risk of becoming tiny, disconnected academic entities lacking the critical mass that can achieve high-quality teaching and research, that can win us high standing both in the region and the outside world. I also call on everyone in the University to consider what links we can usefully build with universities and related institutions overseas. It is the responsibility of each member of academic staff, each department, each faculty and each campus to assess its situation both in terms of its strengths and weaknesses and to identify centres of intellectual dynamism with which mutually beneficial links can be established. I recommend that we should be clear in our minds about what we can offer to the world outside and what we would like to secure from it. Dependent on the answer to that question, we will know how far we are within the mainstream of world intellectual development or how far away we are from it. This strategic question should be answered and dealt with if we are to move forward in the contemporary age.

I am sure that everyone recognizes the importance of members of academic staff being aware of the developments taking place in their discipline and seeking wider public knowledge of the advances they are attempting to achieve in their teaching and research. In this latter context, I am extremely conscious of the increasing need for academic staff to attend more international meetings and establish more scholarly contacts. I assure you, I shall take a deep personal interest in efforts to secure greater funding for such activities. I shall keep you informed of developments in that regard.

Our efforts to build international links should go beyond scholarly contacts. We need to search for partners in establishing joint programmes that can attract students and scholars from different parts of the world. Today there is a virtual ferment among universities to find partners for programme development in a context of reduced government funding and more intense competition for research funds. UWI must be part of this process. We have to find academic friends abroad and forge alliances with institutions that share our objectives and aspirations. But it has to be a two-way process. We should be clear of the benefits that we can offer to our partners. It goes without saying that our offerings are expected to be of a high quality, as we would expect the same from them.

As we open our windows to the wider world, let us pay special attention to our relationships with the non-English-speaking countries of the region and the hemisphere. Let us develop a greater consciousness of the reality that we are part of a multi-cultural, multi-lingual region. Our history has predisposed us to behave as an English-speaking enclave, but in view of the developments which I have cited earlier, it is strongly recommended that we make efforts to enjoy a better understanding of Latin America. At both the cultural and economic levels, our governments are ahead of us in that respect as they have already taken steps to strengthen their relationships with Latin American countries. Senior members of the administration are already active on this front. The three Principals, the Pro Vice Chancellor for Academic Affairs and others have been increasing their contacts with universities in the region and exploring possibilities of collaboration in student exchanges, faculty exchanges and research. We are also beginning to extend our relations with the French-speaking countries and with the Netherlands Antilles and Surinam. I am pleased to bring to your attention that for the first time, the Consortium Graduate School in the Social Sciences, located here on the Mona Campus, welcomed two students from Haiti. We hope that this is the beginning of a trend and that more colleagues in the region will join us as lecturers, researchers and students. I am also happy to note that the Faculty of Arts and General Studies has approved a proposal that all students entering the faculty without appropriate qualifications in French or Spanish should take a course in one of these languages as part of their programme. I hope that this worthy example will be emulated by other faculties.

I should also mention that we are trying to find sponsors for a Latin American House where the culture of our Spanish-speaking neighbours can be shared through lectures, seminars, books and film and can also serve as a meeting place for visiting staff and students from Latin America. I hope we can make concrete progress with this idea during the course of this academic year.

We are also aware that distance teaching can be an effective vehicle for extending our reach into the world. There are good possibilities that UWIDITE can become involved in international teaching where UWI courses are offered in universities and colleges in other parts of the world. The encouraging responses from overseas to our plans to establish summer schools in Caribbean Studies and introduce programmes in multi-cultural education suggest there is a good overseas demand for UWI courses. Furthermore, we are working with the Commonwealth Fund for Technical Cooperation in developing a number of short courses to which we can attract students from other Commonwealth developing countries in Africa, Asia and the Pacific. For example, we are already well advanced in planning specialized courses in plant tissue culture, solid waste management and gender studies. We hope to add to this list in the period ahead.

Quite apart from earning additional income for the University, which is most welcome in these difficult times, there is another side to welcoming students from other parts of the world. It gives our own students an opportunity to broaden their horizons through interaction with them and through the cross-fertilization of ideas that takes place. This is bound to enhance their personal growth. Let me say that the University sees the creation of opportunities for personal growth and intellectual enrichment for both staff and students as a central item on its agenda. That is why we have been pursuing the introduction of exchange schemes and intellectual enrichment programmes such as the Facing 2000 Lecture Series that has brought to the Mona Campus some truly outstanding men and women who have excelled in a number of disciplines, among them have been four Nobel Prize winners. I hope to see this programme extended to our other two campuses. Indeed, although the lectures have attracted good audiences, I wish to encourage all staff and students to take greater advantage of them in the present academic year and beyond. I hope that we can upgrade and expand the cultural activities that take place on campus. Furthermore, my senior colleagues and I continue to attach the greatest importance to the improvement of library and bookshop facilities. We are sensitive to the importance of a good intellectual infrastructure for the growth of both students and staff.

I have not in this address covered many other topics which I would like to encourage you to think about. For example, I believe the University should seriously address the new role and importance of the humanities in our work, notwithstanding the imperatives for strengthening our programmes in science and technology. In that connection, I see a need for expansion and upgrading of our already sizeable programmes in mass communication.

I also want to remind you of all the things that we need to do to make our University more cost-effective, both the administrative and academic services. Academic salaries have improved, particularly on the Mona Campus. But we need to reflect this improvement in greater cost-effectiveness, high productivity and a high quality of service to the community. If we are to sustain our claims for internationally comparable salaries, we have to maintain internationally comparable work, both in terms of quality and quantity. I hope that this is not a general phenomenon, but I am concerned about examples that have been brought to my attention of extensive outside work being done by members of staff. According to the accounts I have received, it is reaching a stage where it could be detrimental to academic performance. It is necessary that we move promptly and forcefully to check this trend. We cannot sustain a case for comparable salaries or satisfactorily discharge our responsibilities to the communities that we serve by part-time academic involvement. I intend to raise this issue at the relevant University committees in the near future.

This opens up the general issue of the quality of service that we give to our clients, namely the students and the wider community. As I have indicated before, we have to become more service-oriented and customer friendly. There are a number of areas calling for serious review; among them are our admission procedures which appear to the public to be protracted and time wasting and give a bad impression to incoming students. We have to be more vigilant in the timely marking of examinations and the prompt publication of the results. We have to deal more effectively with students' problems and demonstrate a greater attitude of caring. We have to pay more attention to our alumni and our outside supporters by keeping them well informed of our activities and by prompt reporting of any funds contributed to us.

At this stage, I underscore the warm welcome which the University Registrar gave to Mrs Gloria Barrett-Sobers, who has recently assumed duties as University Registrar designate. I hope that very soon we shall appoint a new University Bursar. Once again, I express the University's appreciation for the services rendered by Mr Byron Robertson and Mr L. B. Smith who have recently retired from the posts of University Registrar and University Bursar, respectively.

I also wish to say a brief word about staff development. Recently we have received assistance from several sources which open up new opportunities for our staff. These include grants from the Canadian International Development Agency (CIDA), the Leverhulme Trust, the Ford Foundation, and donations from other governments and private sources. I hope that action will be taken immediately to set up Staff Development Committees on each campus so that every member of staff can take full advantage of whatever opportunities are open in his or her field. Contrary to popular belief, we are in a good position with regard to staff development. I look forward to staff taking advantage of them.

Let me make a few comments about the financing of the University's development. We should all recognize that development requires increased resources and that the latter can only come through the exercise of hard choices. Increased resources for higher education mean less for something else in a situation where the pool of resources is slowly growing, if at all, because of such modest economic growth. Governments and peoples realize the importance of investment in education. Communities as a whole have to decide what they will forgo in order to provide the additional resources needed for the expansion of the University. A new alliance is called for between the government, the private sector, non-governmental organizations, parents and students to make a combined effort to provide the University with the funding that it needs. It is a difficult thing to do in difficult times. But we have to bite the bullet if this region is to advance economically and socially. In particular, we are expected to keep at the forefront of our thinking the many thousands of young West Indians who are waiting for a chance to enter the University but are unable to do so at the present time because of limited facilities. If we fail this generation of young people, if we fail to respond to the human resource development needs of this region, we would be setting back the pace of progress, perhaps irretrievably. Let us not allow short-term considerations to cloud our vision and sap our will.

Colleagues, students and friends, I close by reiterating our mission to be one of achieving excellence in all of our fields of endeavour. The demands of our time press hard upon us. I have no doubt that we can meet them fully. Let us recall the central element of our mandate, which is to unlock the creative potential of the peoples of this region. That will take strong commitment and discipline. As the West Indian Commission Report reminded us recently, the West Indies can secure a place in the world of the future if we can develop a highly educated, well-trained, entrepreneurial population. That is the truly modern equivalent to the wealth of the West Indies.

Chapter 2.3

Address by the Vice Chancellor to the UWI Community

At the Start of 1993/94 Academic Year

Members of the University community, I am grateful for this opportunity to address you at the beginning of this academic year. I am particularly glad to see new students in the audience, and some of my comments will be directed to them. At the same time, I welcome returning students and greet my academic and administrative colleagues.

In an address such as this, there are many different issues that come to mind. However, I shall restrict myself to three main themes. I want first to speak to you about some new developments concerning arrangements for student welfare.

I would also like to share with you some thoughts about what the UWI should be doing for the people of the region.

Finally, I want to look at the UWI's response to some of the major changes that are sweeping the world, as these changes will inevitably have profound effects on the Caribbean.

Some Recent Developments in the University

Since I last addressed you, the University has taken concrete steps towards improving the quality of student life. One result of this is the appointment of a Pro Vice Chancellor, whose main responsibility is student relations.

Dr Marlene Hamilton has this portfolio, as well as that of alumni relations. It is no mere coincidence that student and alumni relations are now linked. We feel strongly that our alumni are among our most valuable assets. If we are to look forward to a strong alumni body, it stands to reason that we need to ensure that our students leave here with a feeling of satisfaction, attachment and affinity.

We have long recognized the importance of student welfare and tried within our limited means to attend to it. However, its importance has been accentuated by the introduction of cost-sharing. Effective this year, students are being asked to pay significant fees rather than a cess to the government.

In the circumstances, we felt that it was necessary for there to be an office within the University which deals with the development of policies and measures to provide advice and assistance to students having financial difficulties because of the fee system.

With the establishment of this office – which I repeat is a policy office – students can expect help on their campus on such matters as how to access bursaries and loans and how to go about getting a job to help meet their expenses. Such help will not come directly from the offices of Student and Alumni Affairs, but rather from the offices of

Student Services or their equivalent which are operating at each campus under the policy guidance of Pro Vice Chancellor Hamilton.

Quite apart from the matter of fees and expenses, I also know that students have concerns that are not necessarily financial and for which they need to receive the ear of the senior administration of the University.

I can assure you that you have such an ear in the Campus Offices of Student Services, guided by the Pro Vice Chancellor for Student Affairs and Alumni Relations. I say this with confidence because, in her short term of office as a Pro Vice Chancellor, Dr Hamilton has already established an excellent relationship with the student body. It is truly refreshing to see the genuine enthusiasm with which she approaches her job of trying to find ways to make student life here more fulfilling.

A mentorship programme that was introduced last year as a pilot project at the Mona Campus is only one example of several projects which she has spearheaded. I understand from Dr Hamilton that this project is to be extended to other campuses once the necessary discussions have taken place with staff and student representatives.

On the administration's part, we are making every effort to become more responsive to the needs of our students and the wider Caribbean community which we serve. We are doing this in several ways. In the first place, we have been making several important changes in the administration, designed to improve our efficiency and the quality of services delivered.

The area of human resource management is one which has been targeted for special attention. What we are trying to do here is to ensure that we can attract, retain and develop the calibre of staff required to maintain high academic standards.

I want to emphasize to you the student body that the University is here to be of service to you. In this context, it is our job to be attentive to your needs and keep you supplied on a timely basis with information and advice necessary for you to function effectively as part of our community, and we shall do so with courtesy, as well as with genuine concern for your welfare. If we are falling short in these areas, it is a deficit which I, as Vice Chancellor, am determined to eliminate.

And I shall be asking my senior colleagues to continue to take special steps to improve our performance in this regard.

While I am on the subject of courtesy and caring, may I point out that it is our collective responsibility to eradicate acts of discourtesy and harassment taking place on campus. I think particularly of the disgraceful practice of sexual harassment, which is beginning to rear its ugly head. I call upon all members of the University to work together to stamp out this practice and to discipline its perpetrators.

We are also in the process of introducing a system of student assessment of courses. This system is a standard procedure in many universities throughout the world.

We are introducing it at this time because it is one way of ensuring that students, who are our primary clients, receive the highest quality education. I should stress here that the assessment of a course is a multi-faceted exercise.

To arrive at a balanced and fair evaluation of the quality of our teaching, we are putting in place several measures, of which student assessment is only one. Another is the establishment of staff development units, or their equivalent, to help academic staff upgrade their teaching methods.

As we seek to improve the quality of our work by introducing new systems and new approaches, inevitably, there will be dislocations – periods when we may appear to be making some major mistakes at both the individual and institutional levels. Such changes inevitably give rise to doubts and anxieties. I fully understand that, in solving old problems, we may often create new ones in their place. I hope, though, that none of this would affect your commitment to progress.

I ask for your patience, your understanding and your cooperation. What I can say is that there is no turning back because the world will not wait for us to catch up. It is counterproductive for anyone to try to halt or reverse new processes simply because they may be different from the way we have been accustomed to doing things.

The University cannot make itself a prisoner of the past. If we do, we shall become progressively less relevant, with all the negative consequences which flow from that.

UWI's Role in Regional Development

I turn now to the second area on which I wish to focus today. This is the nature of the University experience and the role it should play in preparing our students for assuming leadership in the future.

Many people are still uncertain about the value of a University experience beyond the acquisition of a degree. While there are certain social realities that encourage a focus on certification, one ought to be mindful that more and more universities are being called upon to justify their existence as servants of society.

At this time, our Caribbean societies need far more than men and women who have been certified as having passed the necessary examinations for degrees. If that were the sole *raison d'etre* of this University, we could be accused of turning out one-dimensional people who are insensitive to the totality of the human experience and to the peculiarities of the Caribbean experience.

In today's world, people too often want ready-made answers without undergoing what Sheridan termed "the fatigue of judging for themselves".

I strongly feel that students should leave the UWI with a capacity for intellectual rigour, with an enquiring mind and with a commitment to creating a better society, rather than simply with a fixation on making a better living.

Our countries progressed to independence and have attained certain levels of well-being, largely because there were men and women of high ideals who were concerned with the common good rather than solely with their individual and personal satisfaction.

I cannot accept that men and women of high ideals are a thing of the past. It is my firm conviction that this institution must set as one of its primary goals the nurturing of an ethos and an ethics that would place the well-being of our countries and peoples above the satisfaction of consumer tastes for luxury goods. This University is obligated to provide our students with a compass and help them to develop a critical mind so that they can pilot their own lives on a route that will lead to a better country, region and world, as we move into the next century.

The century ahead is shaping up to be perhaps the most challenging era that the world has ever experienced. And the message which the new century is presenting to us is "Learn or perish".

In centuries past, when our world was not as complex as it is today, universities could claim to turn out educated and cultured persons. We can no longer guarantee that – or even lay a vague claim to such an achievement. What we can and will do is provide an introduction to learning strategies and methods. It is best practice to equip our students with the means of discovering their full possibilities and potential. That, quite simply, is the true meaning of education – to draw out that which is inherent in the individual and set him or her on the path of knowledge.

We do this because we are in the midst of what has been termed an information revolution.

As John Naisbitt wrote in his book *Megatrends,* the world is drowning in detail but starved of knowledge at a time when we have perhaps more educational institutions and more information than we have ever had in our history.

I read a report recently which pointed out that, in one day's edition of the New York Times, there is more information than any single man or woman who lived in the sixteenth century had to process in the whole of his or her life.

The report further stated that the total quantum of information doubles every five years. I want to add yet another morsel to that. Every year, 850,000 new books are published. Therefore, a big problem is navigating one's way in this vast sea of knowledge and literature.

We are indeed experiencing an explosion of information which, unfortunately, does not equate to an explosion of knowledge. It is simply impossible to teach everything that needs to be learned for the student to be considered an educated person. The individual must himself have a thirst for learning and see it as a continuing process.

In essence, a degree is merely a door to that largely untraveled world of knowledge. A degree is not a destination in and of itself. It follows then that education should teach not only what time and resources permit. It should go far beyond that to give us an appreciation of what we do not know. Hopefully, students will recognize the importance of seeing knowledge as a continuing process, not merely an activity to be undertaken for a fixed period of time.

Even those who view a degree purely in terms of its utility for getting a well-paid job should be mindful that the technological changes taking place are increasing the frequency with which one is obligated to change jobs over a career.

The well-known Ontario report entitled "People and Skills in the Global Economy" has pointed out that the frequency of job changes is likely to treble from two changes per career to six to seven changes.

If you leave this institution understanding this concept, I will conclude that the University has succeeded in its mission, which is to provide the key for fertile minds to open doors towards the vast possibilities for discovery and adventure that are there waiting to be accessed.

To help our students to find pathways to their own explorations, we have resolved to find ways and means of providing intellectual enrichment on all of our campuses, and whenever possible, at our University centres in non-campus territories.

This programme has already started with a distinguished lecture series, which has, over the past three years, brought to the Caribbean 33 very distinguished speakers from many parts of the world. Among these speakers have been five Nobel Laureates, Pulitzer Prize winners, distinguished professors, scientists, writers and other scholars. They have come from top academic establishments in the world, as well as from the private and public sectors and the non-governmental community.

We certainly intend to build on this programme and to identify other ways of bringing to the UWI the finest minds who can engage us in discussions and provide new insights and perceptions for reflection by the University and the wider community.

The lecture series is at present centred at Mona, with some lectures being beamed via UWIDITE to university centres in the region. We are working to extend it, to our other campuses, as well as find additional means of providing intellectual stimulus at all our campuses and centres and into the wider community. I urge you to attend these lectures throughout the year. They are always advertised. Look out for the advertisements under the caption "Towards the Year 2000".

This attempt to expose our students to some of the best minds in the world is, I believe, an important strategy in making this University and its graduates relevant in the world of the next century, which is just six years away.

This broad-based approach to education is essential if we are to take our rightful place in what is increasingly becoming a borderless world characterized by swiftly changing technology and instant communications. We must simply accept the necessity to function in a global community, where parochialism has no dividend. In the global community, we should always be prepared for encounters with the best minds and the best capacities.

We are seeing a situation in which countries are jostling for positions and gearing their human resources for the challenges involved.

As a result, in every country, politicians and business leaders are looking closely at the nature and quality of education.

Students are demanding more of their lecturers. They have a right to expect to be properly prepared by the tertiary system to find productive employment. The whole matter of academic obsolescence should be seriously addressed. It is therefore strongly recommended that lecturers ensure that the courses they offer are up to date. There can be no excuses for outdated information and for the use of sources that are no longer regarded as authoritative. Knowledge is changing rapidly, and our staff must ensure that students get the best available information and guidance.

I believe that our academics should always be guided by the thought that the teaching profession is perhaps the highest of all professions. It is the profession enabling optimism and passion that is passed on to our young people. It is the profession that can motivate our youth to lift themselves out of the morass of mediocrity and, by so doing, move themselves, their country and their region forward.

We should be sensitive to the fact that the winds of change are sweeping through the region. Political barriers are coming down. Economic situations are changing. What does all of this say to us? If we listen closely, we will hear a clear message – that the UWI is obligated to either engage itself in this transition or fall behind.

UWI's Response to Regional and Global Changes

The third and final point on which I wish to speak concerns the necessity for us to wake up to the fact that new regional scenarios are unfolding. With the ending of the Cold War, we are obliged to take hold of the potential of a region of much larger dimensions than that of the English-speaking Caribbean.

Other countries in the region that are much larger than us in terms of land area and population will increasingly tend to become new centres of economic activity. They are moving to position themselves to take advantage of globalization of the world economy. Far from eliminating poverty, globalization could widen the gap between rich and poor countries if the latter fail to build their knowledge base.

We are now at a moment of challenge and opportunity. We must do all that we can to use this moment so that our options can be enlarged.

All available evidence points to the wisdom of strengthening relationships with our Latin American and Caribbean neighbours, if we are to seize the opportunities that can become available to us.

Let me mention only one or two basic facts. The Spanish-speaking Latin American countries together have a population of 355.7 million. This does not include Brazil's 153 million Portuguese-speaking people, many of whom speak Spanish as well. The combined gross domestic product (GDP) of the countries of Latin America is over US$1 trillion. Some of the economies have begun to experience significant economic recovery. It is worthy of mention that four Latin American nations, namely Argentina, Chile, Colombia and Mexico, are attaining nearly 6% annual growth in GDP, and that trend is expected to continue.

This economic turnaround will have major implications for hemispheric trade and investment. What it also means is that increasingly, if we wish to expand our trade, economic and people-to-people links with these countries, we should view them as our close neighbours in a multi-lingual region.

It is quite clear that Spanish can no longer be viewed as a choice but as a necessity. It should be given almost equivalent ranking with English, and the University must point the way. All of you should be determined to leave this institution with a working knowledge of Spanish, otherwise, you will be failing yourself, your country and your region.

I am pleased to see that CARICOM governments have taken the initiative to move towards such an association. However, looking beyond the Caribbean, and to the wider world, it is apparent that we need to gain some competence in Asian languages, including Japanese, Chinese and the languages of India.

Japan is already at centre stage and should be increasingly targeted as an area for trade, investment and tourism. China has been growing at a particularly rapid rate over the past few years. Indeed, China is achieving growth of three to four times the world average. That is a market which, as we approach the twenty-first century, we may ignore to our great disadvantage.

Demographers also tell us that over the next century, India will emerge as the largest country in the world in terms of population. We have kinship ties with both China and

India. It is wise to put these kinship ties to use, bolstered by language capability, to build economic and functional ties with these two great countries.

In many ways, finding our niche in the world economy represents the most formidable aspect of the development challenges facing the CARICOM region today. The challenge is formidable not so much because achieving our goal is beyond our reach, but it is so because of the psychological and other barriers which the region must overcome to develop a comprehensive, integrated and strategic approach to penetrating the world market.

After surveying the situation, one of the University's responses has been to work out, under our Lomė IV Programme with the European communities, bilingual graduate programmes with the Pontifical University in the Dominican Republic. The graduate programmes focus on agricultural diversification, natural resources management, economic development, international business and public sector management.

These will be joint programmes that will start with immersion courses in language and then provide options for students to take courses at either University. We are also thinking of attachments to government ministries, private firms and other organizations, where students can secure work experience in a language other than their own. The intention is to extend this joint arrangement to a Haitian University at the appropriate time.

I wish now to direct my closing remarks to the student body in particular.

You are about to embark on, or you are in the process of, a multi-year relationship with this campus. At the end of that period, each one of you should emerge as a textured person, an individual who is committed to improving the quality of life of others in your sphere of influence or action. I appeal to you to work assiduously towards that end.

As a major catalyst for change, the University should ensure that despite the inevitable problems of limited resources and conflicting priorities of faculties and campuses, that its output should be human beings who have developed intellectually, ethically and spiritually, with values based on a grounding in West Indian culture.

Your experience as a part of this community should equip you to lift yourselves above the limitations of cultural exclusivity and national insularity so that you can function effectively as a Caribbean person with a cosmopolitan outlook.

Beyond that, I urge you to take the social and economic development of the Caribbean as your cause – our collective cause.

I urge you to pay attention to recent developments which pave the way for UWI graduates to work in West Indian Islands other than their own without a work permit. What you will then have is (to use the late Norman Manley's memorable phrase) "A wider field for ambition".

We need people like yourselves to stay within the Caribbean and thereby maximize our potential as a region.

As I said earlier, it is precisely for that reason that the UWI was set up, that is, to develop our own leadership, to produce a cadre of committed men and women who are part of the West Indian experience. If you choose to seek your fortunes elsewhere, then our countries could well be forced to continue the historic trend of importing management.

Let us decisively reject the harbingers of insularity, purveying pettiness and chauvinism, trying to create divisiveness out of diversity, unable to see the wider picture, insensitive to the beckonings of our age, preaching a message that is past and totally out of tune with the character of the contemporary era. More than ever before, we in the University must show vision and take the high road with bold, innovative thinking, marshalling our respective disciplines to provide Caribbean society with a holistic view of where we stand in the world and where we can go.

We cannot afford to fail in this task.

I urge you to wear the mantle of being a West Indian with pride. We have much to be proud of, and our collective achievements have put us on the world stage, far outdistancing the achievements of countries much larger than our combined populations. I also ask that, while we recognize our differences from country to country within the West Indian conglomerate of countries, we also pay attention to our uniqueness and celebrate our similarities.

Let us resolve to get to know each other and to use that collective knowledge of self to build our bridges into the wider world. Let us make the passion for progress a habit, not an unfulfilled ambition.

Let us reach out together into the wider society to make a difference in our local communities, our countries and other regions.

I close on this note of exhortation, and wish for you all a successful year and a renewed commitment to the mission of this University of ours.

Chapter 2.4

Striving for Excellence

Address to UWI Students – Faculty of Social Sciences, Mona, Thursday, March 18, 2004

I am pleased indeed to have this opportunity to share some thoughts with you on the subject of excellence. This is a subject on which I have been reflecting since I was a teenager many decades ago, and which continues to engage my attention. Despite this long engagement with the issue, I cannot pretend to have any answers. Indeed, there may be no answers capable of general application. Everyone has to find his own path but sharing insights and experiences may help all of us in our own assessment of how we can attain success as professionals and, ultimately, be better human beings.

I suppose that a starting point for this enquiry could be the motivation of our own educational and career choices. In making those choices, we are all conditioned by our circumstances and aspirations, sometimes driven by a chance event. For example, when I was about to enter sixth form, I came across in a friend's library two books on economics by Nobel Prize winner Sir Arthur Lewis. I was fascinated that a West Indian was writing on a subject that sounded so interesting, although I knew nothing about it. I borrowed the books, struggled with them, understood only a few points, but they were sufficient to spark my interest in the subject. I was essentially an arts student, but I was bored with the traditional offerings in subjects such as literature, languages and to a lesser extent history. I approached my headmaster and asked him whether I could register for economics and study it through a correspondence course. He was adamantly against the idea at first, but finally relented, if I also agreed to do some of the traditional courses. This was enough of a challenge to spur me on to work hard. Ultimately, I did rather well in my examinations. That choice set me on my course when I was to go later to the London School of Economics. I discovered that self-tuition was dangerous. I had then to unlearn several things that I had taught myself, but by then, I had got sufficient of it right to know that this was going to be a lifetime preoccupation.

My first observation is that I hope in choosing your subjects, you were driven by a fascination with them and a yearning to know more. If you have been choosing courses because they are reported to be easy to pass, that is, the lecturer has a reputation for marking easily; or you do not have to do much reading and other preparation for it – think again. If you are not being stimulated by the problems which the subject addresses, by the controversies which it has generated and by a general desire to know more about it, you are probably exercising a wrong choice and are unlikely to reach the top in that field.

One of the characteristics of most disciplines – in the social sciences, perhaps more than many – is the tendency of the focus of intellectual enquiry to not change when new issues come to public attention. When I was an undergraduate in the 1950s, public concerns were still focused on the problems of recovering from the Second World War, the avoidance of the recurrence of the Great Depression of the 1930s which had spread through the entire world economy, the coming to Independence of former colonies and the consequent economic challenges. This was reflected in our own curiosity as students, even if sometimes the teaching had not quite kept up with it. But other Third World students and I read and discussed the issues extensively, particularly the question of decolonization. That knowledge served us in good stead – perhaps not much in our examinations – but in making career choices after graduation, especially in continuing with graduate work.

The world today is experiencing more convulsive change than five decades ago. Accordingly, the agenda has changed. The economics – indeed, the social sciences – students of today are confronted with major issues, such as globalization, poverty and its eradication, crime in all of its manifestations, human resources development, the development of social capital, international migration, the environment, communicable diseases – to name a few. These are of immediate concern to the Caribbean and to other Third World countries. If you are not reading about them and discussing them inside and outside of your classes, take a reality check. It is an essential preparation for the life that would face us. Relevance and the propensity to contend with change are the essential ingredients of achieving excellence. Get on board if you are not already there.

One of the features of current problems is their complexity. Any of the topics that I have just cited are multidisciplinary, requiring the blending of knowledge from several disciplines. This alone poses a challenge for interaction with persons from a variety of disciplines other than one's own. You need to make inter-disciplinary discussions a regular practice to have a better understanding of current problems. Excellent teaching also calls for teamwork to identify practical approaches to problems. These teaching strategies are increasingly becoming a feature of courses at our universities. However, it is recommended that you reinforce your teaching by organizing team study appropriately and discussing how best to work in teams with your colleagues and the students themselves. Looking back, I think I learnt more in group discussions with other students than I learnt in class. Many students miss this golden opportunity, preferring just to hold on to what they have picked up in classes and from their own studies. They are often perplexed when other students do better than them in examinations and in later life. The exchange of views helps to achieve clarity in exposition and obtaining a more rounded understanding of problems. Find time to have discussions and learn to be a good listener. They will add to your performance.

I would like to extend this point by saying that given the realities of globalization, you should get a good understanding of how students in other parts of the world are thinking. That is almost an essential precursor for dealing with them in the practical world where issues such as the exchange of goods and services and how they are financed will come up for attention. I have often described the tertiary education institutions as "windows on the outside world". Through our own intellectual activity, we can bring our societies to achieve a better grasp of what it takes to compete internationally, and in some instances, to work together with people in the rest of the world.

This is a major undertaking, but one which we are obligated to harness if, as institutions and as countries, we are determined to move ahead in an increasingly competitive world. I have no doubt that we have the brains to hold our own in the world. But we need to develop, more than we have done so far, the drive and the determination to reach the top in the fields of endeavour where we can develop a competitive edge.

I would suggest that we start among ourselves, initiatives to improve mutual understanding by more regular inter-campus dialogue among students on key contemporary issues. This will take organization and money, but that can be within our reach. We can extend it as opportunity allows to students in other institutions in the rest of the Caribbean. As we put the machinery in place for such exchanges, we can as opportunity allows add students from outside the Caribbean. I strongly encourage you to think about this and see what action you can take to make it a reality.

I am assuming that you are already talking to students from other tertiary institutions in Jamaica. If you are not doing so sufficiently, I urge you to step up your efforts to involve them. What is important is that you broaden your outlook while giving them an opportunity to do the same.

While on the topic of outside links, let me repeat a theme to which I have referred on several occasions. In our multi-lingual region, the achievement of excellence includes the attainment of language competence in languages other than English, particularly Spanish. I have for years been throwing out the challenge of making Spanish your second language. It is indispensable to our building stronger links within the broader region and the hemisphere. It is often pointed out that as small countries, we need to create space for our abilities in the world. Language competence is one of the routes towards filling that space. In my own work in Latin America, I often felt constrained by my inability to communicate in Spanish. This will become more and more indispensable as we move further towards trade and economic cooperation with other countries in the hemisphere, such as Cuba, the Dominican Republic, Peru and Chile and those in Central America.

The way the world economy is developing, it is not too fanciful to project that in the period ahead, we shall need to master the languages of countries such as China, India and Japan.

I have painted a rather broad canvas, without covering all of the ground, to illustrate the multi-dimensional nature of the challenges of excellence involving the attainment not only of technical skills but also of personal attributes and an enhanced sense of the world around us. I close with the simple observation that whatever aspect of the challenge one tries to pursue requires hard and sustained work and the exercise of discipline. I keep remembering some of the words from my old school song: "the prize to the one who earns it, let this be our golden rule, endeavour enhances merit, and the slacker is folly's tool."

Let me thank you once again for the opportunity you have afforded me to share some personal thoughts with you on this occasion and to wish you all the very best for the future.

Chapter 2.5

Challenges Facing the UWI for the 21st Century

Presentation at the University of Sheffield Conference on
Change in the Higher Education Sector, Port of Spain,
Trinidad, October 7, 1995

Salutations

I think that all of us here today are cognizant of the rapid and fundamental changes
occurring in the world and their implications for our individual countries and for the
Caribbean region.

Knowledge has become the central ingredient for economic growth and development.
In the Caribbean, we are all aware of the need for greater applications of knowledge
to modernize the traditional sectors of economic activity and develop new ones. The
strengthening of the knowledge base requires a large stock of tertiary graduates and a
vastly expanded effort in research and development.

Increased Access

I do not have to elaborate before an audience such as this how far behind we are on
both counts. It is well known that the gross tertiary enrolment ratio in the region
is less than 5 percent compared with the average for middle income developing
countries of 16 percent to 17 percent. In the field of science and technology, we are
too far behind. One indicator of this is the University enrolment in engineering.
At the University of the West Indies (UWI), about 6 percent of our students are in
the Faculty of Engineering. In the new technology age, we should be aiming at a
substantial multiple of that.

We know from the high ratio of qualified applicants to places that there is a large
unmet demand for higher education. The demand cannot be filled by the conventional
route of on-campus education due to resource limitations. Many of the students whom
we are trying to reach cannot, for one reason or the other, attend the University full-
time. Indeed, we are already witnessing the phenomenon of a high proportion of part-
time students, some of whom are registered as full-time. For instance, at the Cave Hill
campus, some 70 percent of student registrations are part-time.

We shall have to adjust our programmes and methods to cope with this situation.
The present intention is to do so through mixed-mode – a combination of distance
and face-to-face teaching. We also need to introduce a regular summer semester and
extend the practice of modular courses. To take these steps, we are obliged to resolve
intellectual, pedagogical and technical problems.

One of the problems with distance teaching is that students get only limited opportunities for co-mingling with other students that many of us regard as a fundamental aspect of a good higher education. Furthermore, some subjects such as laboratory disciplines are less amenable to the distance mode than others. The distance educational system also favours arts-based courses, thus constraining the objective of achieving a better balance between arts-based and science-based programmes.

We have not yet fully addressed the issue of getting distance teaching accepted as an integral part of the academic programme for both on-campus and off-campus students. This requires that staff not just accept distance teaching as part of their contractual responsibilities but develop an enthusiasm for it and creatively tackle some of the pedagogical problems involved.

Shifting Disciplinary Boundaries

New modes of programme delivery also have to take into account shifting disciplinary boundaries. Technology and intellectual developments are leading to the clustering and even fusion of individual disciplines. Scientific advances in areas such as biotechnology, materials science and natural products have drawn upon more than one discipline. Environmental studies cross over disciplines spanning several faculties. In the social sciences and humanities, the study of poverty and issues of social change and social policy are also multi-disciplinary, as are questions of educational policy and multi-cultural education. In the humanities, the fields of cultural and area studies are of a similar character.

More than ever before, the University of today has to acknowledge and promote these inter-linkages and synergies by the greater use of team teaching. In addition, universities need to inculcate more of a problem-solving orientation in courses. Universities should have organizational structures that deliberately encourage students to follow broadly based programmes and take a more holistic view of their areas of special interest. Much of this line of thinking is now new. As a young faculty member in the 1960s, I was much impressed by the argumentation of scholars such as Lloyd Brathwaite and Lloyd Best, who argued forcefully for this kind of breadth in academic work.

UWI has begun to respond to these intellectual developments by reducing the degree of specialization required for the undergraduate level. But only a modest beginning has been made. Until we achieve greater integration of our departments and faculties, we shall not make significant progress with this matter. In the end, what matters are resources, and unless the structures favour resource pooling, the scope for integration will be decidedly limited.

Competition

Basically, entire organizations have to gear themselves to be on the cutting edge of academic developments to be internationally competitive.

It was not too long ago that some sectors in the University were expressing the view that we had a monopoly over higher education in the region. That was not factually correct, witnessed by the large number of young West Indians who were attending universities abroad.

Because of distance technology and computerization, competition from other universities is now virtually on our doorstep. The presence of our colleagues from Sheffield is merely one manifestation of that. We shall, I hope, discuss the pros and cons of competition. It is a reality of the new technological age. Among the questions we should ask ourselves is – what are the areas in which we can export higher education services to the rest of the world?

Competitiveness means several things. First, we have to be more cost-effective so that we can deliver a competitively priced product. Second, we have to improve our style of programme management, paying meticulous attention to delivery dates and time for lectures, courses, programmes and examinations. Third, we should introduce systematic arrangements for programme evaluation. Fourth, we need to pay more attention to the marketing and presentation of our courses. These requirements are anathema to the more traditionally minded. But this is a wake-up call. We are close to the 21st century and should not enter it with the predispositions and habits of previous centuries.

Globalization

International competitiveness is merely one facet of the phenomenon of globalization, which is affecting the higher education sector at an increasing rate. Many universities are trying to shake off their parochial stance and to view themselves in a global setting. The slogan "think globally, act locally" is becoming more and more the guideline for action by institutions. Small institutions are merging to achieve a larger critical mass and economies of scale. Others are entering into consortia, partnerships, networks and similar arrangements for resource pooling. Educational franchising, whereby institutions allow others, on the basis of clearly defined conditions, to deliver programmes with their certification, is becoming a growing practice across the world. We should respond to the new situation and see what niches we can identify for ourselves. We should deliberate upon the inter-institutional arrangements that are most appropriate to the development of niches.

Partnerships and Networks

We have so far considered that we should advance the internationalization of our programmes through cooperative and link arrangements with other universities.

In the past, we have had faculty, departmental or individual scholarly links with other universities. The long-standing arrangement with the University of Wisconsin in agriculture is one such example. More recently, the development of an Executive Master's Degree in Public Sector Management on the Mona Campus with Monash in Australia and the London School of Economics and Aston University in Britain is another illustration. These will no doubt continue. But University-to-University arrangements extending over several faculties of the entire University may tend to become more and more the pattern.

In the Caribbean, we are establishing several bilingual joint postgraduate degrees with three Universities in the Dominican Republic, and hopefully with one in Haiti covering subjects such as economic development and reform, public sector management, international business, natural resources management, agricultural diversification and information technology.

We are ready to work with other Caribbean universities along similar lines. Conversations are also going on with universities in the Group of 3 (Colombia, Mexico and Venezuela), in Chile and in Brazil.

In Canada, we have already in place cooperation agreements with five universities. The agreement with the University of Toronto is the most active. We are also members of the Association of Atlantic Universities and Colleges. In the United States, several agreements are already in place or are being negotiated. In the United Kingdom, we have link agreements of long-standing, some are being reactivated and new ones are being considered.

We have limited contacts with the rest of Europe. This is clearly an area deserving of attention. Our traditional contacts in Africa are virtually dormant, and here again, we need to move actively, especially with the new situation in South Africa.

Asia is an area deserving of great attention, particularly India and South-East Asia. Malaysia is turning out to be an attractive area for student recruitment purposes. We have 100 medical students from Malaysia at Mount Hope, and we could enrol more students if we had the space to accommodate them.

Adapting to Change

Overall, it is strongly recommended that the UWI promotes itself as a centre for innovation, continuously searching for opportunities to introduce improvements and new courses, pushing ahead with research – and research and development. These are the bases on which we can seek to mobilize additional resources from our governments and from other public and private donors. We should aim to be viewed as the centre of dynamism for the region stretching out into different parts of the world.

In pursuing this new image, we shall have to ask ourselves a number of fundamental questions. For example, should we aim to teach as many courses as we are providing? Might we not be better off securing some courses on distance from other institutions, while we provide them and others with some of our own? How do we reconcile the primary need to attend to the research needs of the region while aiming to score in the wider world? How far do we need to change the culture of our institution from one of leisured reflection and measured response towards a fast-moving entity vitally engaged with the society and the wider world and unconstrained by tradition?

Universities tend to be conservative institutions that place a high value on continuity. However, we should avoid being too much a prisoner of the paradigms of the past. The UWI has not been unresponsive to change, but undoubtedly we have to quicken the pace of response. Most of us are aware that if we do not, this will increase the likelihood that other institutions, both local and overseas, can pass us by.

Part of the new image to which the University must strive is greater financial independence. The principle of more economic tuition fees is almost universally accepted, although much work remains to be done to improve the coverage and terms of student loans. Income generation is also accepted in principle, and projects are beginning to emerge in areas such as summer schools and consultancy. Our fundraising programmes are getting into stride. Given the very modest outlook for economic growth in the region and the claims of the other parts of the education system, it is unlikely that we shall get much more additional resources from our governments. The ball is in our court, and we must rise to the challenge.

If we accomplish all of the tasks that are before us, the UWI of the 21st century will be a significantly different institution than it is now, containing elements listed below, some of which I do not have the time to discuss:

- Larger registrations of off-campus students than on-campus students.
- Mixed-mode teaching for both sets of students.
- Strong links with other tertiary institutions.
- A substantial graduate school with a dynamic and relevant research agenda, attracting support from a variety of public and private sponsors.
- A strong programme of continuing education reaching out to the various sectors of society.
- A diverse range of internationally competitive programmes backed by partnership and networking arrangements.
- A decentralized decision-making structure and overall substantially strengthened management systems.
- A significantly more student-friendly institution.
- Greater financial independence and accountability.

If the UWI can embody these features, we shall enhance our position as a powerful agent for change in the region, fulfilling even more than we do at present, the mandate passed on to us by our founders.

Chapter 2.6

Productivity and Efficiency Issues in UWI

Some Working Notes – Regional Symposium on Tertiary Education Financing, Barbados, November 21–24, 2005

The issues of productivity and efficiency have been a recurring theme in discussions of the University of the West Indies's (UWI) operation. The issues have assumed added significance due to the financial constraints facing the institution and the greater focus on its competitiveness *viz-a-viz* other local, regional and international providers of tertiary education.

These notes provide a brief comment on:

- The problems of measurement
- The current situation of the UWI, as revealed by available productivity information and movements in operating costs
- Suggestions about improving the present situation

The Problems of Measurement

One of the principal problems encountered in discussions of productivity change is to arrive at acceptable indicators of change. In the standard economic literature, labour productivity is measured by movements in output per person hour, while at the macroeconomic level, total factor productivity is represented by changes in real gross domestic product (GDP) per head of the working population. However, it is questionable whether these definitions can be applied to a University. The output of an academic institution is judged not by its contribution to value added for the economy as a whole but rather by indicators such as the number of graduates, differentiated between undergraduate and postgraduate students, the level of research activity, and the income earned from contractual research and other associated undertakings. On the input side, it is questionable that University staff – even if confined to academic staff – should be treated as an undifferentiated mass of workers.

One is therefore left to fall back on some rough indicators that have to be interpreted with caution. Similar reservations can be expressed in relation to operating costs that do not capture significant non-monetary costs arising from teaching, research activity and community service. Regarding staff costs, it is often unclear whether they are defined as salary costs alone or include non-salary benefits such as study and travel grants, sabbaticals and health care.

With these qualifications in mind, it is instructive to look at available information on workloads, research activity and financial costs.

Teaching Loads

Available data on staffing workloads are patchy and irregular, compared to what obtains routinely in comparable universities in countries such as Britain, the United States and Canada with which we compete for students, donor funding and hopefully – looking towards the future – more contract research. Despite discussions that have occurred on this matter since the 1980s, the UWI does not have a regular system of departmental and faculty reporting of faculty workload. The continuing lack of transparency on this subject is troubling and deserves immediate and persistent attention at the highest levels of the institution.

Table 1 provides a summary of teaching activities and academic staff for the current academic year. The table indicates that at the Cave Hill Campus, there was a total staff allocation of 176 full-time staff and 200 part-time staff, a total of 276 undergraduate and 75 postgraduate courses were taught in semester 1 and 346 undergraduate and 120 postgraduate courses were taught in semester 2. A rough appreciation of these figures leads to the question as to whether the average teaching load of a full-time staff member was as much as three courses per week.

The data for Mona lead to not too dissimilar questions. There, in semester 1, a total of 538 full-time and 325 part-time staff taught a total of 528 undergraduate courses and 211 postgraduate courses and in semester 2, 585 and 231, respectively. The situation at St Augustine is comparable. There, 435 full-time and 380 part-time staff delivered 606 undergraduate and 194 postgraduate courses in semester 1 and 664 and 203 respectively in semester 2.

Further information on teaching loads at St Augustine, shown in table 2, indicates that in 2003/2004, 50 percent or more of the full-time academic staff taught two courses or less per week. For the campus as a whole, of the 297 full-time staff members surveyed, 198 of them taught 2 or fewer courses. Compared to the general standard applied in many comparable universities overseas of four courses per week, only 10 percent of the full-time staff at St Augustine achieved that level of performance.

The data on courses taught have to be supplemented by information on class sizes and on time spent on course preparation and associated activities. International data tend to be based on average class sizes of 40 students, but account should be taken of the significant variations arising from large undergraduate classes, requiring several tutorial groups that have to be monitored by the lecturer who may even need to organize more than one lecture course. How far it is feasible to utilize present technology for distance delivery is a matter requiring discussion. At the other end of the spectrum, the problem of very small classes in specialized areas may be the reason to implement distance/online delivery on an inter-campus basis to attain the critical minimum size.

The UWI should no longer postpone the articulation and adoption of a well-defined policy on teaching loads and a thorough system of reporting on them. Available now is a wealth of information, some of which is being collected by the University Planning Office that can provide helpful comparative data for drafting a University Policy on the subject. The University owes it to itself, its financial supporters, its students and the public at large, to take immediate and definitive action on this matter.

Table 1. The University of the West Indies: Summary of Teaching Activity and Academic Staffing, 2004/2005

FACULTY	CAVE HILL CAMPUS						MONA CAMPUS						ST AUGUSTINE CAMPUS					
	STAFF ALLOCATION		Number of Semester-Length Course Taught				STAFF ALLOCATION		Number of Semester-Length Courses Taught				STAFF ALLOCATION		Number of Semester-Length Courses Taught			
			SEMESTER 1		SEMESTER 2				SEMESTER 1		SEMESTER 2				SEMESTER 1		SEMESTER 2	
	F-T	P-T	UG	PG	UG	PG	F-T	P-T	UG	PG	UG	PG	F-T	P-T	UG	PG	UG	PG
NON-MEDICAL PROGRAMMES																		
Engineering	–	–	–	–	–	–	–	–	–	–	–	–	78	53	106	72	124	71
Humanities & Education	47	57	115	33	144	45	116	111	217	51	243	64	76	81	191	42	210	41
Law	17	12	19	5	31	13	2	0	3	0	4	0	1	0	4	0	4	0
Pure & Applied Sciences/Science and Agriculture	59	42	63	9	74	14	101	62	85	38	85	26	93	26	114	33	113	33
Social Sciences	34	87	79	28	93	48	129	118	148	87	168	99	51	56	117	36	139	47
Total Non-Medical	157	198	276	75	342	120	348	291	453	176	500	189	299	316	532	183	590	192
MEDICAL SCIENCES	19	2	–	–	4	–	190	34	75	35	85	42	136	64	74	11	74	11
CAMPUS TOTAL	176	200	276	75	346	120	538	325	528	211	585	231	435	380	606	194	664	203

Source: Compiled from Data Obtained from Campus Registries and Campus IT Services.

Table 2. The University of the West Indies, St Augustine Campus: Summary of Distribution of Teaching Load – Non-Medical Full-Time Academic Staff

TIME PERIOD/ AFFILIATION	NO. OF STAFF SURVEYED	NUMBER OF SEMESTER-LENGTH COURSES DELIVERED BY INDIVIDUAL STAFF MEMBERS				
		1 Course or Less	2 Courses	3 Courses	4 Courses	5 or More Courses
SEMESTER I						
Engineering	74	26	23	15	6	4
Humanities and Education	66	16	17	16	13	4
Science and Agriculture	83	29	28	16	8	2
Social Sciences	48	8	27	10	2	1
Other Academic Units	26	21	3	2	0	0
	297	100	98	59	29	11
SEMESTER II						
Engineering	76	27	22	12	8	7
Humanities and Education	67	16	21	18	6	6
Science and Agriculture	67	34	25	8	13	7
Social Sciences	49	13	16	8	9	3
Other Academic Units	26	24	2	0	0	0
	305	114	86	46	36	23

Note: Other Academic Units include entities such as SALISES and Centre for Gender and Development Studies (CGDS) that are primarily research focused.
SALISES: Sir Arthur Lewis Institute of Social and Economic Studies

Quality

An aspect of productivity is the enhancement of the quality of teaching. All three campuses identified teaching quality as a strategic priority. This indicates the continuing support for the development of the quality assurance system, curriculum strengthening, programme rationalization and diversification. Particular attention is being given to the greater use of information and communications technologies, making them a major instrument in the development and improvement of course delivery and networking in the School of Continuing Studies and in collaborative arrangements with tertiary-level institutions.

The Strategic Plan II also pinpoints the need for quality improvement in postgraduate programmes. Some of the postgraduate programmes have tended to function in a tentative and slow-performing way, partly because of capacity constraints. This is reflected, *inter alia*, in low throughput rates and at best *ad hoc* links to departmental research activities. The latter necessarily limits the institutional capacity to build research and analytical expertise for use in the economy as a whole.

The UWI can recognize a special responsibility to maintain thorough surveillance over the quality of academic programming, not only for its own requirements but also as the leader and pace-setter of tertiary education in the region. We have countless examples of the pressures to expand tertiary enrolment leading to a sacrifice of quality. This could well become a more pressing requirement in the period ahead, for the region as a whole.

Research

Data on research are even more sparse, save for highly qualitative references to research activity in the standard annual reports. However, it would appear that more determined efforts are being made to develop research strategies and to put in place stronger institutional support, as vigorous efforts to mobilize resources, both locally and externally, are being made. A good example is provided by the Mona Campus.

Following upon an impressive report done by a small professorial committee on Strategic Repositioning of the campus, five sub-committees were set up to develop agendas for action. One of these dealt, *inter alia*, with improvements in scholastic output. This subject attracted 12 recommendations for action that, along with others, are in the process of implementation. The recommendations for research are focused on systemic and institutional improvements to document research activity and to aggressively seek to attract funds for its implementation. No comparable information is available on the other two campuses. It would be important to get an indication of activities there.

Concerns about accelerating the volume and pace of research activity are illustrated by the information available on the Mona Campus as shown in table 3 and accompanying figures drawn from the analytical report on strategic challenges facing the Mona Campus. The table portrays a picture of stagnation, if not decline, in publications per staff member. It is reinforced by comparative data on scholastic output in seven other

Table 3. Research Productivity of UWI, Mona (1970–2002)

Year	Number of Academic Staff[1]	Number of Publications[2]	Per-Capita Publications
1970–71	222	250	1.13
1975–76	289	184	0.64
1980–81	319	266	0.83
1985–86	300	258	0.86
1990–91	305	250	0.82
1996–97	327	348	1.06
2001–02	439	398	0.91

[1]Academic staff include full-time academics, at the rank of assistant lecturer and above, and exclude associate lecturers and honorary lecturers and consultants in the Faculty of Medical Sciences, who are part-time appointees.
[2]Publications include all publications, except book reviews, conference proceedings, abstracts, technical reports and newspaper articles.
Source: University Calendars and Departmental Reports, Various Years.

universities that indicate that apart from one University (the University of Botswana), the campus is falling behind the others, with the gap tending to widen over time.

One should be cautious of being too critical about the volume and quality of research at the UWI. In practically every discipline, there are high performers producing quality work that is commanding regional and international attention. Staff members are keen to do better so that they can advance professionally and make a greater contribution to the region's development. However, sceptics may continue to call for a closer fit between rhetoric and performance.

One area of reform that is amenable to early action is to institute a more comprehensive system of rewards and incentives. This could go all the way from better support for high performers by the provision of doctoral and post-doctoral students, the development of international academic contacts that will bring opportunities for researchers and their staff to engage in exchange visits that will lead to joint research and publications, for example. The University should be encouraged to target a donor or a group of donors to support a major investment in research capacity, focused on priority disciplines and subject areas. The basic ideas are already in place. What is needed is encouragement at a high level to package them into a major project for financing such development. This meeting can provide further stimulus for movement on the matter.

Costs

Governments are expressing concern about rising University costs of operation in the context of their diminishing capacities to provide additional financial support. Preliminary investigation shows that the UWI's costs do not compare unfavourably with several comparable institutions overseas. It is also evident that serious efforts at cost containment have been made by the University's management.

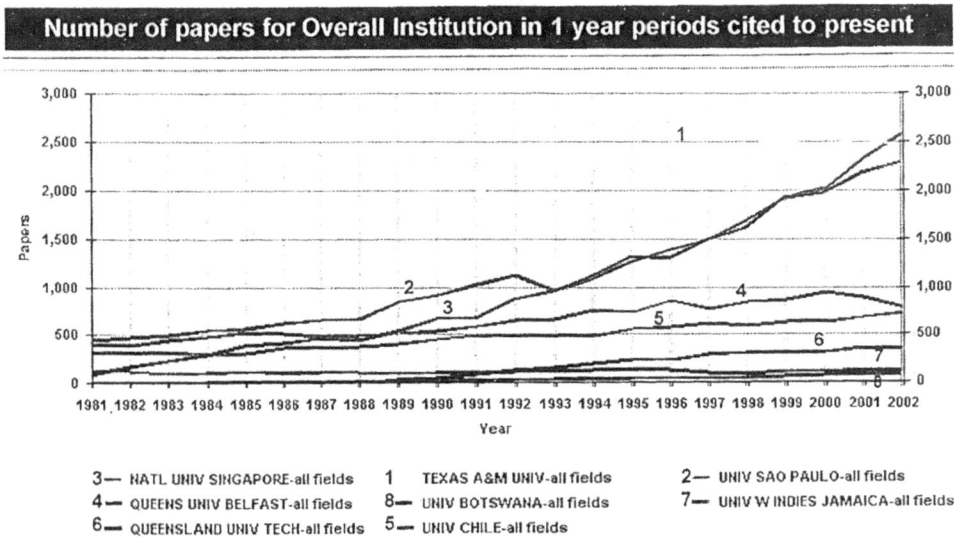

Figure 1. Comparative Scholastic Output of All Cited Papers 1981–2002

Total citations for Overall Institution in 5 year overlapping periods

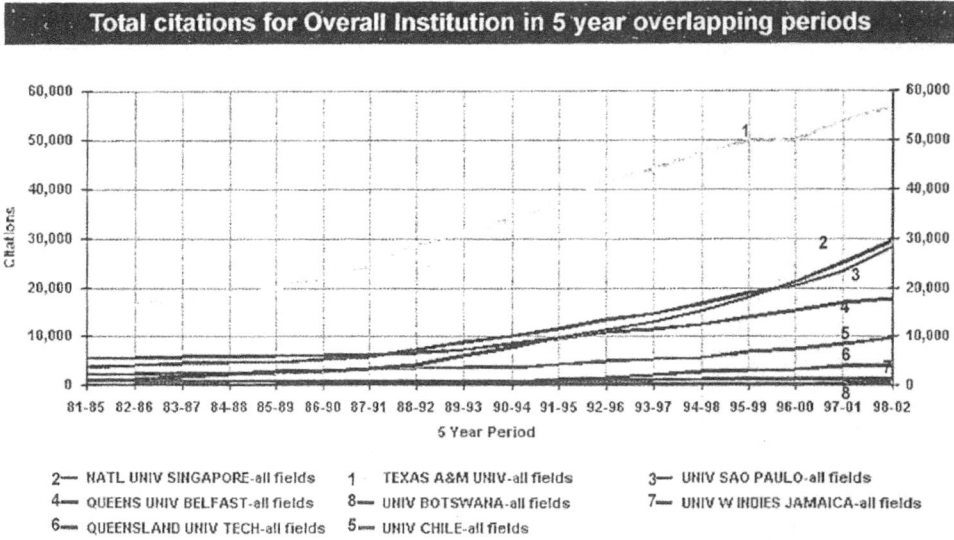

2— NATL UNIV SINGAPORE-all fields   1   TEXAS A&M UNIV-all fields   3— UNIV SAO PAULO-all fields
4— QUEENS UNIV BELFAST-all fields   8— UNIV BOTSWANA-all fields   7— UNIV W INDIES JAMAICA-all fields
6— QUEENSLAND UNIV TECH-all fields   5— UNIV CHILE-all fields

Figure 2. Comparative Citation Levels 1981–2002

Percent of world papers for Overall Institution in 1 year periods cited to present

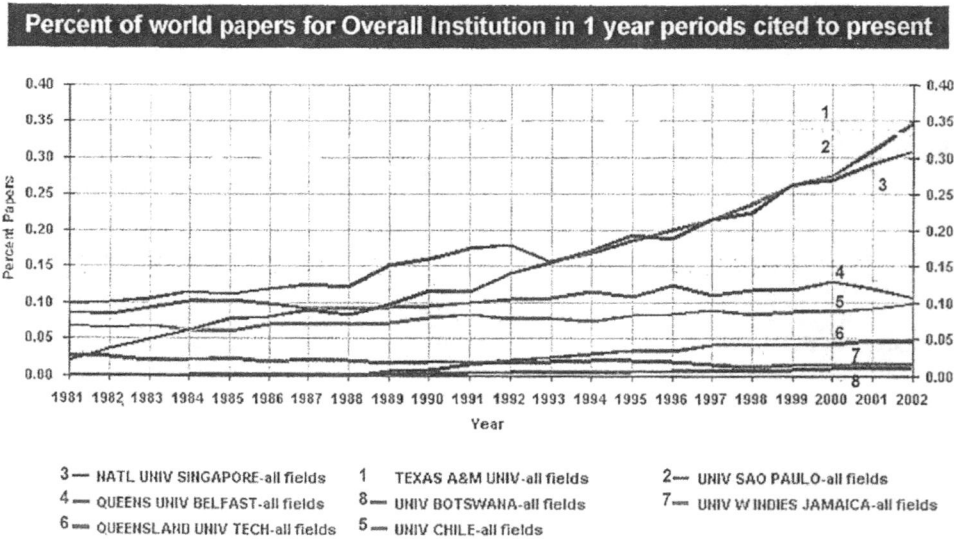

3— NATL UNIV SINGAPORE-all fields   1   TEXAS A&M UNIV-all fields   2— UNIV SAO PAULO-all fields
4— QUEENS UNIV BELFAST-all fields   8— UNIV BOTSWANA-all fields   7— UNIV W INDIES JAMAICA-all fields
6— QUEENSLAND UNIV TECH-all fields   5— UNIV CHILE-all fields

Figure 3. Papers as a Proportion of World Output 1981–2002

Concluding Comments

It is not an over-dramatization of the situation to say that the UWI faces enormous challenges regarding its sustainability and growth. These challenges emanate from the standpoint of future resource availabilities and confronting competition from an increasing list of tertiary providers, both within the region and from outside. Although some advances have been made on issues relating to competitiveness, in particular in the thinking among the leadership and senior academics, there is much ground to be covered. The University deserves the support of regional public and private donors and the international community. The University needs this support to move further ahead with its aim of being a dynamic institution positively impacting major areas of the region's development.

Chapter 2.7

The West Indian University Revisited

Sixth Eric Williams Memorial Lecture, Central Bank of Trinidad and Tobago, June 18, 1988

I am delighted to be back here in Port of Spain. I consider it a significant honour to be invited to deliver the Sixth Eric Williams Memorial Lecture. I have chosen to speak on "The West Indian University Revisited" in order to express some preliminary thoughts on certain issues connected with the future development of the University of the West Indies (UWI).

The University will, this year, be celebrating its 40th anniversary. This provides an appropriate occasion for review, assessment and projection. I am, therefore, gratified to note that public consultations about the University are taking place here in Trinidad and Tobago. I hope that this timely initiative will be emulated by other contributing territories to the University so that we can have a full exchange of ideas on the University and its future.

On September 1, I shall assume duties as Vice Chancellor of the University, having left the institution 14 years ago and the region itself 11 years ago. My long absence handicaps me in speaking about this subject. Prudence will normally dictate that I hold my tongue until I have fully re-acquainted myself with the University and with the conditions in the region to which it is obligated to relate.

I feel impelled to share some of my perceptions with you this evening. I think it is essential that we take action on many of the matters related to the development of the University. Do note that this lecture contains my personal views and do not necessarily represent the views of the University.

The Record of the University

Over the 40 years of its existence, the University has chalked up a solid record as a regional centre for teaching, research and outreach activities. I most sincerely compliment my colleagues for their achievements over the years, despite the many difficulties that we have had to surmount. It is not a chauvinistic remark to say that compared with other institutions of similar origins in different parts of the Third World, the UWI stands out for its stability, growth and resilience. This is in no small measure due to the quality of its staff and students and to the substantial and steady support which contributing governments and external sources have provided over the years.

The University has progressed from a single campus at Mona planned for 600 students to 3 campuses with a total student body of almost 12,000 students, with a School of Hotel Management and Tourism in Nassau, and with University Centres in all 14 of its contributing territories. UWI has graduated a total of some 35,000 students with first degrees, higher degrees, diplomas and certificates.

The research record of the University is equally noteworthy. Every single faculty and department of the University has major publications to its credit, reporting on advances made in understanding and solving important problems, more often than not of the region itself. The research record of the University is reflected in the fact that outside grants – principally for research and related activities – account for over 20 percent of the institution's budget.

A similar situation prevails with respect to outreach activities. University people are to be found in every section of community service: advising governments and serving on their various standing and *ad hoc* bodies; participating and assisting civic groups; arbitrating labour disputes; contributing to the print and electronic media – to name a few examples. It would be difficult to imagine any major event taking place in the region today with which the University would not be associated in one form or another.

Dr Eric Williams, were he alive today, would have taken some satisfaction from the University's achievements. Although it would be characteristic for him to view the institution with an incisively critical eye, and to come forward with innovative ideas, many of the directions which the University has taken over the years were foreshadowed in his seminal speech at the Institute of Jamaica in August 1944 on "The Idea of a British West Indian University".

In that speech, Dr Williams placed much emphasis on the role of the University as an agent for development and for strengthening Caribbean identity. In both respects, the UWI has much to its credit; but it will have to respond to formidable challenges in the years ahead. Of particular importance will be the University's contribution to resolving the development problems with which the region will be faced.

Development Imperatives

The basic challenge facing the countries of the Caribbean is to find and utilize opportunities for vigorous growth, after a decade or more during which several countries have experienced stagnation and even negative growth. This is not the place to engage in an analysis of recent economic performance. Suffice it to say that the Caribbean Community (CARICOM) countries may be moving into the last decade of this century and into the next one, with a serious accumulation of unmet development needs and with a diminished capacity to provide for them.

The Caribbean must take full stock of its reality. More than ever, recognition has to be given to the limited growth potential of the traditional sectors such as mining or export agriculture, partly because of poor international demand prospects, and with respect to petroleum, resource depletion. Even in the case of tourism, where market prospects are better, the outlook for the industry depends upon the region's capacity to diversify both its tourist attractions and its sources of tourists.

Despite all of the efforts that have been made, the region is still a chronic importer of food. The manufacturing sector remains at a rudimentary stage of development. The services sector and the physical infrastructure in many countries require significant rehabilitation and upgrading.

The critical question is: what can be the new sources of growth? Without attempting to provide a detailed answer to this question, I will say that future growth will greatly depend upon whether we can successfully make the transition from a pattern of development, principally dependent on natural resources, to one dependent on human resources and knowledge. This will require a major strengthening of our capacity to acquire, adapt, develop and utilize technology. We have to look increasingly towards science, technology, management and organization, as key ingredients of the development process.

Meticulous attention should be paid to updating the technological content of our endeavours. Greater use should be made of biotechnology in modernizing the agricultural and fishery sectors, and the development of engineering industries oriented towards exports have to be sped up. Information technology should be harnessed for the production of both goods and services. Management will need to be trained, and the entire labour force should be inculcated with values that assign the highest importance to hard work, discipline and achievement, all of which illustrates the considerable gap that separates aspirations from current performance.

No overnight solutions are available. Experience elsewhere indicates that a significant enhancement of technological capability will depend on sustained efforts, lasting perhaps over several decades. But just as one looks back over the last 40 years with some satisfaction, it is imperative to develop a vision of the next 40 years and to begin a response to the prospects and challenges that lie ahead.

Deficiencies in Tertiary Education

The University faces a major task in contributing to the more sophisticated person power needs associated with strengthening the region's technological capacity. At the most aggregative level, in all but one of the contributing territories, enrolment ratios at the tertiary level (i.e. the number of students enrolled at the tertiary level as a percentage of the age cohort 20–24) are currently 5 percent or less. This can be compared with a figure of about 12 percent for Hong Kong and Singapore and over 30 percent for the Republic of Korea, the latter being roughly the figure for a large number of Western European countries and Japan; and over 57 percent for the United States.

In the field of science and technology, the region is far behind. To give one example, according to the UNESCO Statistical Yearbook of 1987, Trinidad and Tobago with a population of 1.1 million had in 1985 a total of 1,226 students enrolled at the tertiary level in science, mathematics, computer science and engineering. Compare this with Singapore, which with a population of 2.6 million had in 1984 over 18,000 students enrolled in those fields. This may be a rather dramatic comparison, but an examination of the available data for other fast-growing developing countries confirms that the region is lagging behind.

The issue which the University and the region will have to face is how to remedy these deficiencies. I suppose one ought to start by seeing how far numbers can be increased through the fuller utilization of existing capacities. I am not on firm ground here, but based upon some recent information that I have seen, it appears that the University is already pursuing and needs to be encouraged to further pursue some important possibilities.

The Expansion of Access

One is to step up the provision of University teaching through outreach activities, particularly in the non-campus territories. Here, the UWIDITE system and the Challenge Examinations can be important vehicles for increasing the access of students to University courses. Governments in the non-campus territories are already making efforts to mobilize resources for first-year and non-degree teaching in subjects such as mathematics, science and management. However, these needs also exist in areas distant from the campuses in the campus territories themselves. There are several such areas in Trinidad and Tobago. We all welcome the initiative taken by the Commonwealth Heads of Government to establish a Commonwealth Distance Teaching Facility that will complement our programmes of distance teaching.

We at the UWI are also engaging in discussions on how student enrolment can be expanded through more systematic networking with existing tertiary level institutions in the region. Virtually all of the contributing territories have one or more tertiary institutions which can be upgraded to provide at least some first-year subjects, including certificate and diploma training in certain fields. Some of these institutions could upgrade their courses to accommodate the needs of second- and third-year students. It is obvious that full advantage should be taken of these possibilities to cut both the cost and time involved in obtaining a University education and bring the University into a closer relationship with the communities that it serves.

It is necessary, however, to guard against the dangers of institutional proliferation. In tertiary education, critical minimum size and economies of scale are extremely important considerations. Experience, even in the Caribbean region itself, shows that it is extremely difficult to provide high-quality instruction on a sustained basis in national institutions operating with the handicap of small teaching units.

It is inevitable that such institutions will find it particularly difficult to recruit and retain high-quality staff if they are restricted to teaching a limited range of general courses with few opportunities for intellectual interaction and with a poorly equipped infrastructure in the form of libraries, laboratories and equipment. The UWI itself is struggling against great odds to maintain its academic standards in the reality of financial constraints.

The idea of consolidating existing tertiary units into a single national institution may be a good one if the new structure is linked to a strong support system. Without the latter, it might end up as a mere exercise in re-labelling. Such support can best come from an institution with experience of local conditions and needs. In any case, it should come from an institution of substantiated academic standing.

I echo the concern of those who have expressed the view that the region is sometimes too easily tempted by access to the facilities of institutions of comparatively low standing. One should not have to make the trite observation that the young people of the region deserve nothing but the best. A second-rate education cannot produce anything other than second rate performance.

One of the services that the University can provide is to assist national tertiary institutions to establish relationships with external academic institutions. Too often, because of a lack of initial information and insufficient local experience, these arrangements fail to satisfy the objectives for which they were established.

A situation can be envisaged where the University develops progressively, systematic arrangements for supporting the delivery of undergraduate programmes at the general degree level by national tertiary institutions. However, to overcome constraints of critical minimum size and economies of scale, it may be advisable to organize a regional network of mutual support. The national institutions concerned could aim to achieve a measure of complementarity in their programmes of study. They could engage in regular staff and student exchanges. They could also co-operate in developing teaching materials and conducting examinations. In other words, serious thought needs to be given to the feasibility of developing a regional tertiary network with the UWI as the main support and feeder institution.

I would like to encourage CARICOM Governments to arrange for a comprehensive feasibility study of such a network. I feel certain that the University would contribute fully to such an effort.

Over the next 40 years, who knows whether the UWI might not emerge as principally a "topping-up" and graduate institution at the apex of a network of associated undergraduate colleges? This is an exciting prospect, but for it to be realized, the foundations have to be carefully laid by thorough preparatory work and planning.

The expansion of access can also be facilitated by the introduction of semester and credit systems and the establishment of a comprehensive summer school programme. These are all currently under study at the University, and I am hopeful that positive recommendations will be forthcoming shortly.

I am particularly interested in a summer school programme, not only because it will increase access for West Indian students but also because it can provide a useful source of additional income if students from overseas can be attracted to the University. There are a number of fields such as history, literature, linguistics, the social sciences and education, where overseas students of West Indian origin or persons who are working with West Indian communities abroad, including teachers, might wish to attend the UWI. A well-developed summer school could be beneficial to both the faculty and regular student body of the University and enhance the international standing of the institution.

Improvements in Curriculum and Orientation

Apart from the increases in numbers which have to be achieved, thought should be given to curriculum reform in light of changing development requirements and educational advances worldwide. On previous occasions, I have expressed my belief that the University needs to introduce a core programme of work for all of its students that exposes them to science, technology and management disciplines.

In particular, I feel that the aim should be to make every student computer literate. I should add to this the need to adopt a problem-solving approach in courses and to provide students, wherever appropriate and feasible, with hands-on experience. This leads me to mention the growing importance worldwide of sandwich programmes involving alternating periods of study and work and of "fast-tracks" where students can complete their degree work in a comparatively short period of time by year-round attendance. This is relevant to what I have just mentioned about the introduction of a credit system and summer school.

The crux of the matter is that the UWI is obligated to consciously create a greater development orientation into its teaching, trying, among other things, to reduce the gap between the world of study and that of work. This will necessitate changes in the content and orientation of programmes and courses and improvements in work habits. The entire range of academic activities should give prominence to the importance of hard work, discipline and achievement. The University should view itself as a pacesetter for society as a whole in promoting high productivity and cost-effectiveness.

Let me hasten to recognize the point made by those who are concerned that such practical approaches run the risk of turning the institution into a degree factory. This is not a problem unique to the UWI. Universities in many countries face stiff competition for resources and public questioning of their relevance, making strenuous efforts to improve the practical orientation of their teaching while endeavouring to build on their reputation as centres of reflection and intellectual innovation. The plain reality is that if universities are to function simply in the style of medieval cloisters characterized by leisurely intellectual activity, they should expect no more than medieval levels of resources for their programmes.

Research

A principal test of an institution's capacity to reconcile the practicability of its work with intellectual depth and innovation is the quality and the local and international reputation of its research. As I have said before, UWI has a good research record and could do more if more resources were available.

The strengthening of research and postgraduate studies is a need common to all of the University's campuses and faculties. The University will not be able to retain high-quality staff and students, let alone undertake the investigative work required for problem-solving in the region if regular budgetary provision is not made for research and postgraduate work. Nearly all of the University's research is financed by external sources, and postgraduate programmes are being maintained on a shoestring basis.

The Caribbean needs a stronger and more sustained research effort by the UWI to focus on research development, if the technological thrust about which I spoke earlier is to have any chance of success. It is necessary for research and development to become a regular part of the operation of all sectors of the economy.

Enterprise and Technology Parks

One way in which the University can give some impetus to these activities is by establishing enterprise and technology parks in a triangular partnership with governments and the private sector. I have in mind centres where management training packages can be provided for local business as well as a range of support services, such as data processing, financial analysis and accounting, laboratory testing, market research and design, engineering and feasibility studies. Enterprise and technology parks can be of particular value to start-up enterprises. Based on the experience elsewhere, the establishment of a cluster of such services can serve as a magnet for the location of companies, particularly those utilizing state of the art technologies.

There is already some institutional capacity for the establishment of enterprise and technology parks in the region, two examples being Cariri here in Trinidad and Tobago and the Scientific Research Council in Jamaica. However, I feel sure that these and other similar institutions would welcome a greater involvement by the UWI, with as many faculties as possible associating themselves with the effort. Here again, the UWI can conceive of itself as the principal feeder institution for building up a network of mutually supporting organizations and companies working in the field of research and development. I recommend that the governments of the region consider the UWI as the feeder organization for such initiatives and activities.

Caribbean Identity

I turn now to the second dimension of Dr Williams' original concerns about the University, namely the development of Caribbean identity.

The idea of Caribbean identity is sometimes dismissed as a sentimental notion associated with past attempts at Federation. It is true that when Dr Williams spoke about the University over 40 years ago, he discussed the evolution of Caribbean identity in terms of Federation. But much more fundamentally, the idea of Caribbean identity has to do with survival in a complex and rapidly changing world.

The basic question is: how can the tiny states of the Caribbean survive and retain their shared social and cultural values in a world becoming less heterogeneous under the impact of satellite communications and more intricate partly because of the emergence of major economic groups and new centres of economic power.

Can the Caribbean states aspire to be more than Lilliputian entities in the twenty-first century, with some standing in the international community? Without the underpinning of a solid grasp of their history, their culture and the articulation of a world view, will it mean anything to be called a West Indian in the years to come? Or for that matter, will it mean anything to become a citizen of Trinidad and Tobago, Grenada, St Lucia and so on? What will those designations represent to those who use them and to the outside world?

I pose these questions not to provoke tendentious debate but rather to present the challenge in a reflective and analytical manner, with the understanding that much still needs to be done, despite all of the work accomplished over the last four decades. In some respects, the Caribbean appears to be more vulnerable now than it was in the early 1960s at the time of independence. I hope that I am not misreading the situation, but there seems to be less certainty about our place in the world, what we are trying to achieve, and how to set about securing that place.

In a certain sense, we have also become more inward-looking, preoccupied with immediate local problems, and setting aside the larger picture.

This is to some extent understandable because many countries in the region have been going through really difficult times. But we cannot keep our eyes closed for too long. The world outside is changing rapidly, and we need to get a better grip on those changes and see what they portend for our future.

Personally, I would like to see active programmes on regional and world affairs in all of our campus and non-campus territories. In addition to the formal academic training provided by the Institute of International Relations and the Faculties of Social Sciences, there is considerable scope and opportunity for a regular series of open lectures, seminars, panel discussions and short courses. Given the available new technologies, the University should be encouraged to produce a wider range of programmes and publications targeted towards the non-specialist public. The University should mobilize and develop regular radio and television material on regional and global issues for its ongoing programmes of public education. I shall be inviting contributions, in particular from external sources, to develop some of these activities.

Area Studies

In this context, the University needs to go further in developing area studies. Considering the extensive relations which the region has with the United States and Canada, it is surprising that we do not yet have a regular programme of American studies. One can make the point even more strongly concerning Latin America, from which we are still relatively isolated. It is not too visionary to look forward to the day when Spanish can become the second language of our institution, thereby giving our students greater access to the richness and diversity of Latin America. I hope that we progress along this road by increasing academic contacts with Latin American universities, arranging more exchanges of staff, students and publications and more systematic co-operation in research.

Concluding Remarks

In this rather cursory overview of some possible directions for the University's development, I have strayed over a rather heavy agenda of issues that is by no means exhaustive. A recapitulation of the discussion is as follows:

- Regional networking and development of national tertiary institutions.
- The establishment of semester and credit systems and a comprehensive summer school.
- Curriculum reform, by providing students with greater exposure to science, technology and management disciplines, and to a practical orientation.
- Substantial strengthening of research and postgraduate studies, with an emphasis on research and development activities.
- Extending the work on international affairs and area studies as part of the University's ongoing contribution to the evolution of Caribbean identity.

In order to respond adequately to these challenges, the University needs a substantial increase in its resources. The governments of the region are already stretched in providing support for the University. However, I urge them to fulfil their present financial commitments and particularly to clear their arrears of contributions. The arrears outstanding to the University reflect themselves in a run-down physical plant which endangers the maintenance of academic standards. Governments are aware of the concerns about faculties such as medicine and natural sciences, the general overcrowding, and the poor state of the library system and student amenities. If the University is to do its job, these and other deficiencies have to be remedied immediately.

I shall be encouraging the University to launch a public appeal for financial support in all of its contributing territories as well as overseas.

Let me start here and now in Trinidad and Tobago by asking you to respond as much as possible when the appeal is launched. These are difficult times. Yet, it is because they are difficult that we have to make the extra effort.

In general, I very much hope that through the appeal, the University and communities as a whole can come closer in tackling the region's manpower and development problems and in trying to realize its full potential.

I hope that our alumni will play a leading role, not only in fundraising but be more involved in the development of the University as a whole. A fair percentage of our alumni, many of whom are abroad, are well-placed to make part-time or occasional contributions to the University's teaching, research and outreach activities. Systematic machinery needs to be set up for this purpose. I hope the occasion of the anniversary will encourage a beginning along these lines.

May I end by once again expressing my great pleasure to be here. I pledge my efforts – and I am sure that I can do likewise on behalf of my colleagues at the University – to enable the further growth and development of the University and of the region.

Chapter 2.8

Address on the Occasion of the Opening of the Alister McIntyre Building, Cave Hill Campus, October 2009

Mr Principal, Members of the Academic Fraternity, Ladies and Gentlemen.

It is always a pleasure for me to come to Cave Hill. I have been visiting here from the earliest times and have always admired the steadfast and tidy way in which you have executed your plans and programmes for development.

As you know, from the beginning, Cave Hill had both regional and sub-regional mandates. The first mandate was to establish and develop a Faculty of Law to serve all of the countries which contribute to the University. The second mandate was to pay special attention to the degree and non-degree needs of the country members of the Organisation of Eastern Caribbean States (OECS). In both of these respects, you have been a good and faithful servant. You have endeavoured to satisfy not merely the minimum standards for accreditation, but you have built programmes of quality with the best academic staff available for the purpose. In academic affairs, as in other fields of endeavour, we should hold fast to the precept that the race is not for the swift but for the strong.

Turning to the honour that you are conferring upon me today, I cannot begin to describe how gratified I am about this act of generosity on your part. In designating the building for the study of Caribbean Integration, you are pointing towards the root of my being a West Indian.

For me, Caribbean Integration is not a mere subject for academic discourse or a field for professional advancement. It is an exploration of my own *raison d'être*. My commitment to West Indian integration began at the age of five, when I was able to read Grenada's only newspaper, The West Indian, produced by the well-known federalist, T. Albert Marryshow. The motto of the newspaper was "*The West Indies must be West Indian*". From those early days, that precept has constituted a fundamental part of my life.

As for the study of integration itself, my intellectual journey began with a four-hour conversation with William Demas, which took place at the West Indies Trade Commission in London in 1956. The conversation could not be completed because Sir Garnet Gordon, the then Trade Commissioner and Demas' boss, needed him to deal with an urgent matter. I was late for a class at the London School of Economics and had to hurry there.

The friendship that began with Demas blossomed into a long-term relationship which was reflected in his writing, the justly celebrated book on the economics of small countries. In 1964, while I was visiting Columbia University in New York, I was invited by Economic Commission for Latin America and the Caribbean (ECLAC) to spend some time at their office in Mexico City writing a piece on the Caribbean. That turned out to be a long essay on "Aspects of Development and Trade in the Commonwealth Caribbean", which was published by ECLAC in 1965. In many ways, Demas's and my publication were close relatives. He took the initiative to have my piece discussed at an informal meeting of government technocrats at the Institute of Social and Economic Research (ISER) at Mona where Lloyd Best and I were the co-rapporteurs. The meeting was not well attended. Demas and Arthur Brown took responsibility for virtually all of the discussion. Out of that discussion emerged a decision to recommend to governments the negotiation of a free trade agreement. A parallel process had emerged at Dickenson Bay in Antigua involving the governments of Antigua, Barbados and Guyana. These two initiatives converged in a series of official encounters that led to the Heads of Government Conference in Barbados in October 1967, where the Caribbean Free Trade Association (CARIFTA) was born.

The discussions from that meeting led to a decision to sponsor a series of university studies on integration. Out of this emerged the renowned Dynamics of West Indian Integration by Brewster and Thomas and valuable papers by contributors such as Beckford and Girvan. The integration process was greatly enriched by these contributions, even though immediate results were not forthcoming. What they did was to establish integration as a major field of research and study in the University. For one reason or another, the momentum generated in that period has not been sustained. If I may offer some gratuitous advice, it is time for the University to return to that mission. This building could be regarded as an important step in the process.

To return for a moment to my relationship with Demas: at the Barbados Conference, the two of us began what was to become a continuing conversation with Sonny Ramphal on the development of the integration movement. Over the years, the three of us collaborated on a variety of initiatives that reached their peak with the West Indian Commission report *"Time for Action"*, which Ramphal chaired and piloted every step of the way. The disappointing outcome of the Commission's report is well known in the region, and I do not need to dwell on it. One of the reasons why the required technical work has not continued at the scale and pace anticipated was the absence of an intellectual home to develop the concept. Today, a new opportunity beckons to make this right.

In saying this, I do not wish to belittle the contributions who have come from established institutions such as the regional secretariats. A place is needed where more reflective work can take place to reinforce and supplement whatever is emerging from the established institutions. It is in that spirit that I commend the idea to the University authorities.

On the subject of integration itself, we are at an important crossroads with Caribbean Community (CARICOM). For the most part, market integration has run its course. The focus of governmental attention and technical work should move towards the integration of supply, including the development of a public/private sector institutional framework for cooperation and collaboration among large and small companies and firms involved in the production of goods and services for supplying intra-regional and extra-regional markets. This is not the occasion to elaborate on this subject, but I leave the matter for further reflection by those involved in the integration process.

I think I have said enough to indicate that a major job of work needs to be done, for which this building can be a home. I am confident that it will fulfil the role which has been conceived for it by those responsible for its construction.

I thank you.

Chapter 2.9

Address – Speaking Notes

Opening of the Alister McIntyre Building, University of the West Indies, Mona, September 2, 2002

Chancellor, Vice Chancellor, Principal, Dean of the Faculty, other members of the University, Ladies and Gentlemen.

My family and I are very moved by the generous gesture of the University in naming this building after me and establishing a Research Group in Public Policy in my name.

Both of these acts have led me to reflect on the evolution of the Faculty of Social Sciences. I continue to have a deep commitment to this faculty, particularly the development of management studies, now largely resident in the School of Business.

Along with many others in the University and outside, I have for long espoused the case for a vibrant programme of management studies as a critical element in the development of local and regional entrepreneurship on which the sustained development of our economies so much depends.

However, I have been a small cog in the wheel to the development of the social sciences. My thoughts go back to my arrival at the Mona Campus in 1960 to teach economics and how unprepared I was for that responsibility. I felt reasonably comfortable articulating the latest theoretical advances in mainstream economic theory and what was then called development economics. When I related these paradigms to the Caribbean – on which my students legitimately insisted – I was in some initial difficulty. Matters were not helped by the fact that I was the only West Indian in a Department of 12. I had to turn to fellow West Indians in another Department of the Faculty – Sociology, where the great Lloyd Braithwaite and the two Smiths – M.G. and R.T. – held sway. Braithwaite took a special interest in me, often setting aside his own work to introduce me to the literature on Caribbean society and to explain concepts in social sciences, unfamiliar to a raw recruit.

At the Institute of Social and Economic Research (ISER) was Lloyd Best, one of the most creative minds that I have encountered in my entire career. As he was also an economist or rather, as he would insist, a student of political economy, he became a natural partner. Among other things, we began working almost immediately on joint papers, two of which saw the light of day into publication. But the informal conversations into the wee hours of the morning were far more important in shaping my own understanding of the Caribbean and integrating that into my knowledge of economic theory. Roy Augier was a frequent participant and provided historical dimensions. I suppose I should also acknowledge the contribution of Red Stripe,[1] several bottles of which lubricated the discussions.

Not to be forgotten are the streams of students with whom I came into contact. Compared with the undergraduates whom I had taught at Oxford, I found them to be hardworking and motivated to grasp the relevant concepts.

In the field of business studies, I think back to my early contacts with the Jamaican Institute of Management and with businessmen such as Aaron Matalon and Carlton Alexander, both of whom were strong advocates of the University entering the field of business studies.

One should also not forget the contribution of teachers in the field of management and related disciplines. I think of Gladstone (Charles) Mills in public administration and the late Arthur Brown in public finance and Uriel Salmon in accounting. They laboured over several decades to improve the teaching in their respective disciplines. Further, Charles Mills played a major developmental role in the Department of Government.

I also wish to recall my period at the ISER when the Regional Programme of Monetary Studies was established; it has produced several persons of prominence. Two of them, Professor Compton Bourne and Sir Dwight Venner, occupy critical positions of financial leadership. Others are to be found in the central banks holding senior positions, in universities, in the public service and the private sector.

I make reference to these persons not merely to engage in nostalgia but to remind us that this building belongs to all of them, as it will belong to those who will come in the future. The idea of naming a building after an individual is not to suggest a presumed place in history. Rather, it is intended to be a signpost of where we have arrived and of the journey that lies ahead.

In its first 40 years as an independent degree-granting institution, the University's primary role was to reinforce and extend its original mission to prepare a leadership model for our constitutional independence, establish Caribbean scholarship and develop a reputation as a centre of high-quality teaching and research. Despite the lively controversy on the interpretation of this mandate as far as the social sciences are concerned, the faculty has to a much larger extent, than our critics have recognized, substantially discharged these responsibilities. There is today no corner of the Caribbean Community – in politics, public administration, business, education and other parts of the social sector, in the media, where University of the West Indies (UWI) graduates are not to be found occupying positions of responsibility. In several instances, they are graduates of this faculty or had access to courses here. We have also made a mark in many fields of research.

The mission for the future requires a continuation and consolidation of the original mandate while responding to new imperatives. In the world of today characterized by the phenomenon of globalization, the UWI and its Faculties need to seize the space available to them to become more international in character. In the language of the economist, we have to move beyond the phase of import substitution and displacement and add an export dimension to our work.

International trade and cross-border Investment activities in educational services, especially higher education, has been growing rapidly in recent years, driven by technological advances and increasing world demand for postsecondary education and specialized training. In our own region, we see evidence of this growth. We cannot afford to sit idly by and allow these trends to gather momentum without establishing a place for ourselves in the new order.

Already, the WTO is becoming active in this field. In the context of negotiations under the General Agreement on Trade in Services, it is envisaged that the requests for educational services could come up as early as the first quarter of next year. So far, four countries – the United States, Japan, Australia and New Zealand – have tabled proposals for the liberalization of educational services. Other countries have signalled that they intend to do so, although reservations continue in some quarters about treating education simply as an internationally traded service.

As consumers of education, we have to be vigilant on issues such as quality assurance, certification and sustainability of our local institutions. At the same time, it is my view that there are niches in the international market for higher education services, which we should pursue resolutely and aggressively.

Though I will not go into detail here, I encourage my colleagues to give serious consideration to this matter if they are not already doing so. The Faculty of Social Sciences, in particular the Business School, has a leading role to play in such endeavours. In particular, I hope that the School of Business and the new Research Group on Public Policy will consider assisting the region in preparing for negotiations, and the University in undertaking feasibility studies and market research into the most promising opportunities.

Altogether, I have no doubt that whatever choices they make, the faculty and the University as a whole will contend successfully with the challenges of this century.

It remains for me, Chancellor, Vice Chancellor and Principal, to thank the University once again for the signal honour they have bestowed upon me today.

Note

1. A beer brewed in Jamaica.

Chapter 2.10

National Development

Aspects of the Task Ahead – Address to the Graduating Class, UWI, Mona Campus, February 9, 1980

A visit to the University of the West Indies (UWI) – especially to the Mona Campus – is always a special kind of homecoming for me. I owe a special debt of gratitude for the opportunities that it gave me for intellectual and personal growth. My fourteen years with the University were rich indeed. They filled out my understanding both of this region and of my own discipline. The fact that I stand here today as a recipient of an Honorary Degree and as the Speaker at this graduation ceremony is more a tribute to what the University has done for me than to any special attributes on my part. Nonetheless, I wish to thank the Public Orator for the rather generous things he has said about me with his customary eloquence.

In collecting together the thoughts that I wish to share with you, my starting observation is that we live in an age of unprecedented challenges. The world economy has hardly ever known as much instability as exists at the present time – recession, massive unemployment, inflation, disorderly exchange rates and destabilizing monetary movements. In our own region, as practically everywhere else in the developing world, it has virtually been a battle for day-to-day survival. Economic development has become increasingly elusive, and with that, deepening anxiety about what the future holds.

Despite the serious difficulties that exist, there are substantial opportunities to be grasped. It is well recognized that one of the consequences of constitutional independence is the scope that it gives for the exercise of self-reliance in seeking out and utilizing opportunities for economic development. The task facing this generation of West Indians is to build upon our constitutional independence so that it may yield for all the people of the region more substantial and lasting benefits by way of economic and social advancement.

In the quest for economic and social development, the countries of the Caribbean have to work simultaneously at three levels – the national, the regional and the international. In the brief time that is available to me, I would like to raise a few questions of direct relevance to the national effort. Here, it is evident that the first step is to examine recent experience with a view to deriving appropriate lessons for the future.

I do not need to set out in detail the weak spots in our recent economic performance, which are well known to you, and which you have been experiencing in your daily lives. Some of the main challenges can be described in a single sentence. They are the challenges of inadequate economic growth, inflation, balance-of-payments pressures, the under-utilization of human resources reflected in high unemployment and the brain drain.

Governments recognize that most of these difficulties cannot be overcome unless they can get the principal production sectors of their economies moving again. For the most part, the real growth which occurred over the 1970s was concentrated in the service sectors, principally the government sector. Indeed, in some countries, the government has now become the largest single employer of labour. There is everywhere dissatisfaction with the slow growth and even stagnation occurring in key sectors, notably export agriculture and manufacturing. Although the mining sector has been buoyant in Trinidad and Tobago – though not in Guyana and Jamaica – there is general recognition of the need to increase its contribution to development in all three countries.

Buoyancy in the government sector reflects widespread acceptance of the view that the public sector has a unique and catalytic role to play in generating economic development within a framework of social justice. In recognition of this role, governments in the region have not only expanded their activities in traditional areas, such as education, health and housing. They have also engaged in a wide variety of experimentation in the search for new patterns of ownership in the productive sectors based on more popular participation by nationals in economic decision-making. Examples of such experimentation are the promotion of co-operatives, schemes for worker participation, locally owned and controlled enterprises often involving new partnership arrangements with foreign capital and the establishment of state enterprises.

As a result of their experimentation, governments now have a better idea of the forms of popular participation that are compatible with efficiency and rapid economic growth. Moreover, there is now a greater understanding of the role that institutional change can play in the development process and the interplay that is required between state and individual initiative.

In the Caribbean, because of our peculiar history, authoritarianism and bureaucratic control have been juxtaposed against an absence of social responsibility. Governments are therefore caught in the real dilemma of trying to pursue programmes of social justice which, because of the weak institutional structure in the society as a whole, seem only capable of achievement by an extension of centralization and bureaucracy. We experience all the consequences that this entails through the concomitant growth of political patronage.

Some sectors of opinion in the region have drawn attention to the desirability of according a larger role to individual initiative in economic development. It is possible to see two dimensions to the role of the individual. One is to make a maximum contribution to increasing the production of goods and services through hard work, discipline, thrift and the pursuit of values that stress achievement in a context of equality of opportunity rather than ascriptive criteria – be those class, colour, cultism or ideological compatibility.

The other dimension is to contribute towards the creation of a framework of social responsibility that recognizes the basic rights and needs of everyone in society. A framework of social responsibility strongly suggests that the country belongs to the entire population and not just a few. In other words, if there is a desire to strengthen the role of the individual in society, we should abandon schizophrenic attitudes that involve blaming governments for encroaching too much into economic life while simultaneously defining the task of social justice as the exclusive responsibility of the state.

Today, the Caribbean needs a new infusion of community initiative in crucial areas of national life. Everyone shares the responsibility for running the country. This is particularly with respect to communal services, such as keeping our cities clean, providing and maintaining public and recreational activities, and achieving high standards of social services in areas such as health, education and public transport. Deep-seated attitudes of dependency on governments are a critical bottleneck to a more vibrant economic development and the maintenance of social and political stability.

A related observation has to do with the need to improve our capabilities for self-management. The starting point for such an improvement is the recognition that a community cannot indefinitely absorb more resources than it is producing. Historically, a major feature of our economic life has been the tendency to perpetuate patterns of consumption that could not be sustained on the basis of our production. This is most vividly illustrated in those islands where national consumption has for some time exceeded the total production of goods and services. In other words, not only have these territories not been setting aside sufficient savings, they have also been dipping into the pockets of the rest of the world to finance their excess consumption. It requires no elaborate argument to show that these behaviour patterns are basically anti-developmental. A positive by-product of recent economic difficulties has been the growing recognition that consumption patterns and their associated lifestyles must conform more closely to what our countries can themselves provide.

More generally, there is the need for greater public acceptance of the constraints under which governments and society have to operate. This extends not only to the need for national support of policies of fiscal discipline but also for those relating to income restraint and the management of foreign exchange. Within such a climate of understanding, governments can be expected to pursue more resolute and prudent management of the public sector, and a fruitful basis would be provided for longer-term planning.

One cannot help being struck by the slippage which has occurred in development planning throughout the region. Efforts at national planning began in the region some two decades ago. At that time, Jamaica was being used as a training centre for planning officials from other developing countries. Trinidad and Tobago was then said to have the best statistical base for planning in the Western Hemisphere outside of North America. Mainly through the efforts of their governments, by the end of the 1950s, practically all Caribbean Community (CARICOM) countries had national plans, which contained at least a forward programme of public expenditure extending over a period of years. During the 1960s, some countries improved on those early efforts by producing macroeconomic plans, embodying development targets for the economy as a whole rather than just for the government sector.

Today, only a minority of governments have presented plans even of the modest dimensions of the 1950s, let alone articulated a sufficiently detailed and systematic view about the future development of the economy. At the same time, there is mounting public concern about the slow implementation of development projects, about weakness in project management, including the problem of cost over-runs which in some instances have reached alarming proportions.

The present neglect of planning is partly a result of the international economic crisis that, as I said earlier, has distracted attention from longer-term development issues. In part, it also derives from a certain scepticism about the value of macroeconomic planning that tends to encourage too much attention to model-building and mathematic elegance at the expense of the more practical problems of product preparation, implementation and management.

Governments should not become too discouraged by past experiences with planning. What is required is an adjustment in planning techniques to reflect the experience that has been gained rather than an abandonment of planning itself. Bear in mind that in the absence of a carefully defined economic strategy backed up by a sensible forward programme of government capital expenditure, the population has little to go by in assessing the future and what contributions they should make to it. More generally, a national dialogue on development both within and among CARICOM countries can make an important contribution to generating greater confidence in the economic future of the region.

Within the compass of my limited career, I have had the good fortune of a fair exposure to development experiences in many parts of the world. I have become increasingly convinced of the importance of the human factor in economic development, particularly the need to generate and sustain an atmosphere of confidence throughout society. The more one reflects on contemporary successes and failures, the more it becomes apparent that these cannot be explained by objective circumstances alone, such as resource endowments and international support, whether by way of resource transfers or access to markets. Too much emphasis cannot be placed on the need to give everyone in the society a feeling of involvement and security in making their contributions to national development. Without it, countries risk serious misuse of their human resources with diminishing possibilities for economic and social development.

There are a number of factors that reflect the emergence of a new confidence in the region. Examples are the growth of small businesses, the adjustments that are taking place towards more modest lifestyles, the upsurge in cultural activity with all that this implies for national coherence and solidarity, and the growing involvement of young people in national life. The task ahead is to build on these foundations so that all sectors of society can move together to achieve desired goals.

I have spent most of the time available to me commenting upon some issues in national development. I do not intend to imply thereby that the pursuit of developing opportunities at the regional and international levels can be neglected. Indeed, the linkages between the three levels of action should always be recognized. In particular, it remains my personal view that regional economic integration is an indispensable element for national development in every country of the region. I am not convinced that the economic arrangements within CARICOM are unsound or are incompatible with so-called ideological differences among member states.

An examination of CARICOM within the wider setting of integration experiences in other parts of the world, and in the context of the growing interchange between countries with different economic and social systems, would show that there are no technical obstacles to intensifying the economic integration effort among the countries of the region. This is notwithstanding the political pluralism that is said to exist.

I suggest that the first task in promoting a revitalization of CARICOM is to undertake in each member state a searching appraisal of economic strategy and policy so that the linkages between the national and the regional effort can be more precisely identified. A desire to make rapid progress has prompted too much reliance in the past on rhetoric and intuitive judgements. If each country, as part of its planning effort, were to embark upon an assessment along these lines, a firm technical basis would be laid for negotiations within CARICOM. In its absence, the integration effort will necessarily be fitful and appear at times almost marginal, if not irrelevant.

What West Indians have long recognized is that integration is for us as much an economic as a psychological necessity, in our efforts to build new societies on a basis of common but weak historical and institutional roots, and in the context of a world becoming increasingly complex for small societies. Accordingly, approaches to economic integration have to be constructed that will mobilize the energies of the population in the region not only for conventional acts of economic cooperation but also for collective efforts to strengthen national societies and the development of a Caribbean identity.

These latter considerations particularly apply to the territories of the eastern Caribbean, where the problem of single state viability continues to cause concern. The issues in these islands are not merely that political integration can confer certain economies of scale by way of administration and the operation of common services, important as these may be. It is more fundamentally a question as to whether these territories can by joint action achieve a measure of viability and identity to counteract tendencies towards extreme balkanization that leaves them at the mercy of geopolitical rivalries. This is not a matter of concern only to the eastern Caribbean. The Caribbean Community as a whole has to guard against forces of disintegration that continue to be present, and some might even say, are on the increase.

I have said enough to indicate that a large task awaits you as you proceed to enter the arena of national development. I have every confidence that you will play your full part. I hope that you will feel that sense of challenge and excitement that for many of us sustains our commitment to the region on the basis of undiminished confidence in the future. I am sure that you will eschew the empty pragmatism of the careerist. I know that you will hold fast to your ideals while keeping your feet planted firmly on the ground. Bear in mind the injunction of the philosopher who observed that "it is only in marriage with the world that our ideals can bear fruit: divorced from it, they remain barren".

Let me end by expressing my great pleasure to be here and my deep gratitude to the University for the honour that it has bestowed upon me.

Chapter 2.11

Inaugural Address

To the Vice Chancellor's Roundtable, the Council Room, UWI, Mona, September 15, 1995

I wish to join in the warm welcome already extended by the principal to you, the participants in the Roundtable, and to our guest speaker Mr John Naisbitt.

It is always a pleasure having members of the private sector on campus. It is a signal of the growing interest which the sector is taking in the work of the University, and I thank you very much for that. It is also an indication of increasing interest on the part of the University itself in building strong links with the business community – and I commend my colleagues who are directly involved, most of them being here this morning. May we all find the session today to be meaningful and rewarding and to provide us with a basis for moving ahead.

As for Mr Naisbitt, his fame has preceded him. Most of us who are acquainted with his writings have already discerned him to be someone of encyclopaedic knowledge and profound insights with an ability to articulate them. I am sure that we shall have a stimulating and informative presentation from him.

Our guest speaker will help us focus on global trends which will impact Jamaica. However, we should be equally concerned about our state or preparedness to meet the exciting but daunting challenges of the period ahead.

We are all agreed that Jamaica, and indeed the entire Caribbean, must accelerate the implementation of export-led strategies of development and seek to increase exports by diversifying both product composition and markets. The critical factor here is to increase the profitability and international competitiveness of Jamaican firms.

One dimension of the problem is the overall business environment, about which a good deal of discussion has been taking place. The private sector should endeavour to intensify its dialogue with the government to push for the desired improvements.

At another level is the company response, namely the readiness of companies to begin exporting or to increase existing exports. In this connection, several questions come to mind. For example: how many companies are working on or have completed strategic plans for export growth? How many of them are undertaking market research into new export destinations? Are research and development activities improving existing products and developing new ones?

Are companies planning alliances with local or overseas companies to increase export capacity and international competitiveness?

Is management being trained for an export drive, and at least have the human resource requirements identified?

These are some of the questions to which answers have to be found and decisions made. To postpone them is to opt for marginalization in tomorrow's world. These are network with them that includes Lille in France, Charles II in Prague, a leading school in Japan and Johns Hopkins Medical School in the United States.

The network will provide for undergraduate and graduate exchanges, faculty exchanges and joint research programmes, including the bidding for consultancies worldwide.

I expect this pattern to be repeated in other faculties so that we may offer our students access to the best possible education on a world scale, and we can continue to build our already good reputation in research.

As we succeed with these endeavours, we shall be providing you with high-quality graduates and investigative services where we can draw on personnel and information from leading sources in the world. We are determined that the UWI will make an important input into the growth of profitability and international competitiveness of Jamaica and Caribbean businesses. We have to work more closely in the many areas of mutual interest.

One important part of the next phase is to establish a business school. The time is right for that, and I hope that we can count on your involvement and support as we proceed to that phase.

Let me take this opportunity to acknowledge the important contributions that the business sector has already made to the UWI. Among them are the following.

The Century Club, which is an innovation pioneered by Hon Dennis Lalor and his collaborators, and in many ways, ushered in a new phase of UWI-business cooperation. I am advised that the Club has now 59 members, namely companies that have agreed to contribute J$1 million or more. Some companies have pledged major donations. Here are some examples. I understand that the Carreras Group is donating J$10 million towards a new building for the business programme. Grace Kennedy and Company and Alcan Jamaica have endowed two Chairs and one Chair, respectively. The Bank of Nova Scotia has contributed to the expansion of the Accident and Emergency Unit in the Faculty of Medical Sciences. In addition, there have been grants to the Department of Surgery, provision of housing for nurses and a significant grant from the Caribbean Cement Company to expand the Tropical Metabolism Research Unit (TMRU) building.

Although many persons have been involved with the projects, the principal contributions have come through the initiative of the Hon Mayer Matalon. Scholarships and bursaries have been donated by several companies and some of them with vacation jobs attached. The IBM Initiative for the leadership development of students should also be commended.

This is by no means an exhaustive list, and I thank all the companies in Jamaica who have in one way or other supported different aspects of the UWI's work. I am, in particular, appreciative of the growing list of companies who are sponsoring students. From the University's standpoint, we feel that if we can continue along and extend this path of cooperation, we can make a difference to the Jamaican economy. I am confident that we can succeed.

Chapter 2.12

Notes on Governance and Decentralization

In the Context of the Regional University, March 7, 2008

My remit is to provide some opening comments on the issue of decentralization and the regional university in the context of governance. A great deal of passion has been spent on this issue. This is a larger issue than most people realize. In the limited time available, I shall only touch upon a few points as a basis for further discussion.

The governments of our contributing countries, acting in their capacities as Heads of Government of Caribbean Community (CARICOM), decided in 1989 that the University of the West Indies (UWI) will remain as a regional institution indefinitely. The issue of decentralization has to be consistent with that mandate.

The decision to retain the UWI as a regional institution was made partly on economic grounds and also on the basis of the governments' collective desire to retain international recognition of the high quality and academic autonomy of the University. There was a strong underlying sentiment that UWI should be a major vehicle for the economic integration of the region.

The presence of the UWI as a regional institution has greatly facilitated the establishment of the Caribbean Single Market in the context of the clear movement within the region of university graduates and holders of professional qualifications. In a sense, the UWI has also been provided a protective shield for national tertiary institutions wishing to be treated in the tradition of academic autonomy. In other words, if the history of the UWI was different and we had started with three national universities, we might be considering now whether they should be joined together under an umbrella agreement in academic standards as a building block for the Caribbean Single Market. I will speak of our extra-regional situation in a moment.

The question of academic accreditation has become one of the thorniest issues in international economic relations as countries jostle to gain training advantages with respect to the growing international trade in services. This includes traditional areas such as medicine, engineering, law and accountancy extended to new fields related to technological advances, principally in information technology, such as telecommunications, media, hospitality, entertainment and construction.

The UWI starts off with a good advantage in medicine because of our previous link to the General Medical Council in the United Kingdom. These links are no longer in place, and we shall have to negotiate new accreditation arrangements in an increasingly complex situation. The Faculty of Engineering, having retained its British links, can therefore more comfortably establish its international academic *bona fides*.

As far as non-professional qualifications are concerned, we are in a relatively favourable situation compared to many developing countries because of the ready acceptance of our graduates by top universities in the United States and throughout the developed countries of the Commonwealth. By way of comparison, some of the universities in less developed parts of the Commonwealth enjoy currently only associate degree status. As one Vice Chancellor explained to me, that is the outcome of "political interference and academic conservativism". In both respects, we have to guard our heritage jealously so that we can make our way in the new global economy as it gains momentum throughout the world.

I end with a general observation: we could not have achieved the growth in student numbers that we have secured by retaining only a single campus. The spread of the University into three campuses and having an Open Campus makes an abundance of good sense; however, this should in no way inhibit a regional approach to the development of the UWI. Indeed, we should use the multi-campus structure creatively in the application of new technologies to teaching and research, in conscious efforts to develop a regional ethic as we endeavour to strive successfully for a secure place in the new world as it emerges. It will continue to be difficult to avoid isolationist tendencies, but we need to build strong defences against it and to instil in our staff and students an appreciation of the wider context in which they are playing their part in the further development of this institution.

Epilogue

The analysis contained in the preceding chapters indicates that in the changing conditions of the contemporary world economy, major modifications and adjustments are called for in foreign trade which can become a new engine of growth for the future. This applies not only to the product composition of trade but also to the major trading partners.

In relation to products, it is evident from the experiences over the past several decades that alterations have to be made in respect of several items. With respect to agriculture, it has become evident that less reliance should be placed on traditional lines such as bananas, cocoa, coffee, sugar, arrowroot and cotton as major sources of foreign exchange earnings. This is not to say that whatever contributions can be secured from these items should not be sought. It is rather to suggest that beyond the earnings that they can provide, new sources will be required. The critical issue therefore becomes one of identifying new possibilities involving both products and markets that could provide fresh momentum. Caribbean countries have to embrace recent developments in technology to enhance the value added associated with traditional lines of production. Furthermore, the regional producers have to determine which areas of the global value chain they would like to give focus.

The Caribbean Trade Routes map [see page 149] suggests scenarios which would warrant careful examination. The map illustrates major possibilities that might be developed, both with respect to existing products and new ones. However, the map is not an exhaustive one and seeks only to illustrate some of the important areas that would warrant continuing attention. The region needs to strengthen its negotiating and diplomatic skills to carve out market access for Caribbean goods and services. The trade agreements should take on board the existing and projected capacity of regional producers to supply goods and services on a timely basis and at the level required by the receiving markets. The provisions of these agreements also need to be promoted among regional producers as the uptake of previous agreements has not been as great as one would have expected. They should also signal to producers and governments the necessity of strengthening capacity.

One matter worthy of careful attention is the markets that will become more accessible with the development of the Panama Canal. This would allow the Caribbean new access to markets in Asia and the Pacific, such as Australia, New Zealand, the Pacific Islands, going further to Southern and South East Asia. It is already recognized that countries such as Jamaica can provide openings for the movement of goods and services from the Western to Eastern parts of the globe. The Government of Jamaica as well as other countries in the region have already recognized some of these possibilities and are taking steps to prepare the necessary facilities to support the development of entrepôt trade. This can constitute a major source for growth in exports and employment throughout Caribbean Community (CARICOM).

In the early part of this century, Jamaica and other Caribbean countries provided substantial labour for the construction of the present canal. To be considered are the possibilities that can be developed to expand trade with some South American countries such as Colombia, Mexico, Chile and Brazil, where at the present time volumes of trade are small. To this end, one should add the countries in Central America where there have been long-standing traditional ties and where the scope for trade expansion in goods and services should be carefully explored.

A virtually new area for trade expansion in both goods and services would be the Pacific where present levels are minimal, notwithstanding the relations that have existed since the formation of the ACP Group. Only one Caribbean company has so far invested in a sugar factory in the Pacific, presumably with satisfactory results. But it certainly bears investigation whether further investments could be developed including joint ventures to take advantage of markets in Australia, New Zealand, Japan and South East Asia. Indeed, this could provide a general launching pad for firms of differing sizes developing exports in relation to both products and services.

To take the point further, this suggests that one dimension of the new relations that could develop within the ACP Group is the growth of intra-ACP trade which could be a good candidate for support by the European Union.

Turning to other possibilities for trade expansion within the African, Caribbean and Pacific States (ACP) Group expanded to include the rest of Africa, it is noteworthy that some trade and economic cooperation is already developing between the Caribbean and Africa. This is occurring in West Africa where Caribbean companies are seeking to expand their business in countries, such as Nigeria and Ghana. The prospects in other West African countries are also deserving of careful attention. This is also the case in Eastern and Southern Africa, notably in Kenya and South Africa and in other countries in the sub-region. It should not escape attention that Southern Africa is developing export capabilities in areas such as fashion, music and film where a basis can be developed for joint venturing and increased mutual trade. Such trade relations might give impetus to the strengthening of the integration movement in the Caribbean region within the context of a single market and economy.

In turning to the more traditional areas, it is important also to note that the expansion of trade with the Pacific would also open opportunities for increasing trade with Canada. Indeed, an area worthy of investigation is the extent to which drawing upon traditional relationships with Canada, the Caribbean might find an opening through that relationship towards the Pacific and the entire southern zone. This could well point towards a possible arrangement with the Trans-Pacific Partnership (TPP) to cite merely one of the possibilities that could be present.

The foregoing indicates the need for a major initiative to explore possibilities for trade expansion with several parts of the world where, so far, the Caribbean presence is minimal.

The task will undoubtedly be a major one, but it is certainly not beyond the capability of Caribbean governments, working with the private sector and institutions. In other words, a new era of Caribbean trade and development could be in sight if countries were to combine their capabilities through all the stages of trade development, starting with investigations of the prospects. The UWI and other institutions in the region can

CARICOM Trade Routes Map

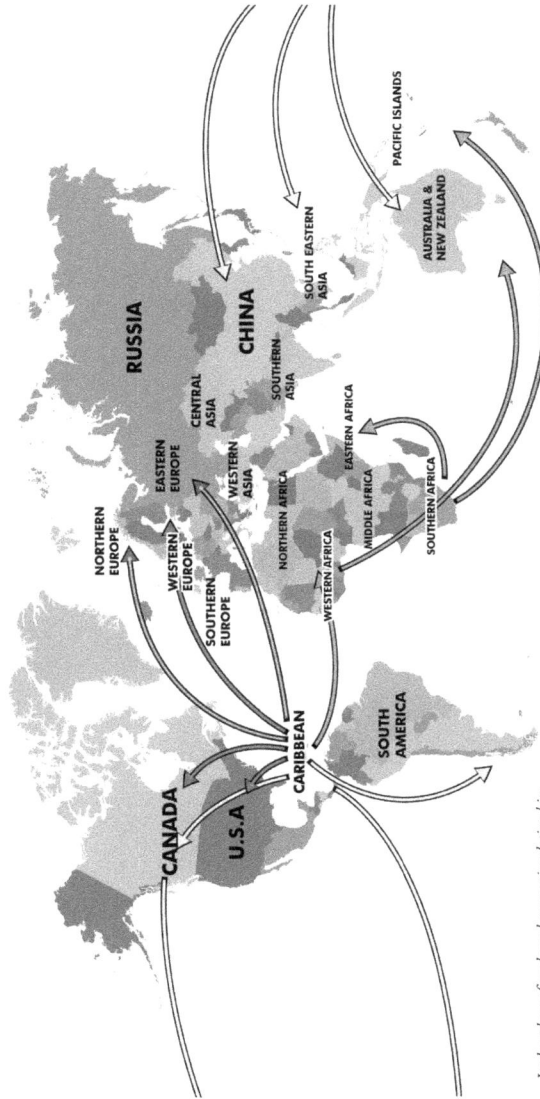

CARICOM Trade Routes:
some possibilities for the future

CANADA

U.S.A

CARIBBEAN

SOUTH AMERICA

NORTHERN EUROPE

WESTERN EUROPE

SOUTHERN EUROPE

EASTERN EUROPE

WESTERN ASIA

CENTRAL ASIA

RUSSIA

CHINA

SOUTHERN ASIA

SOUTH EASTERN ASIA

NORTHERN AFRICA

WESTERN AFRICA

MIDDLE AFRICA

EASTERN AFRICA

SOUTHERN AFRICA

PACIFIC ISLANDS

AUSTRALIA & NEW ZEALAND

In the sphere of trade and economic relationships;
the Caribbean should explore exhaustively all opening for strengthening those links. This should include the following:

○ CARICOM Trade currently focused on Europe, USA, Canada: Continuing emphasis on traditional partners

○ New emphasis on Canada - TPP / NAFTA /China / India (Canada, Other Latin America, Australia, New Zealand, Pacific, Japan, India, SE Asia, China)

○ Further emphasis on Non-Traditional European partnerships (Northern & Eastern European)

○ Development of ACP African links, with special focus on West and Southern Africa new focus on the Pacific (Western, Eastern and Southern Africa, Pacific Islands)

List of Selected Lectures, Addresses and Papers

Sir Alister McIntyre

1. "A First Appraisal of Monetary Management in Jamaica", *Social and Economic Studies*, Vol.10, no.3, 1961, pp. 353–363 (with Lloyd Best)
2. "The Political Economy of the Federation" (with Lloyd Best), *Pelican Magazine*, March 1962
3. "Aspects of Development and Trade in the Commonwealth Caribbean" *Economic Bulletin for Latin America*, ECLAC, 1964
4. "Decolonisation and Trade Policy in the West Indies" (with F. Andic & T. Mathews). 1965 Ed. The Caribbean in Transition, University of Puerto Rico [reprinted as "Some Issues of Trade Policy in the West Indies", *New World Quarterly*], vol.2, no.2, 1966, pp.1–20
5. "The Political Economy of Canadian-West Indian Relations", May 5, 1966
6. "West Indian Membership of the Sterling Area: A Regional View", Proceedings of a Regional Conference on Devaluation, ISER, UWI, 1968, pp.211–229
7. "Studies in Foreign Investment in the Commonwealth Caribbean", ISER, UWI, 1970
8. "Some Economic Issues Arising from the Options offered by the Enlarged European Economic Community to Developing Commonwealth Countries in Africa, the Indian Ocean, the Pacific Ocean and the Caribbean" – Commonwealth Secretariat, March 1972
9. "The Effects of Reverse Preferences on Trade Among Developing Countries", United Nations, 1974
10. "Reflections on the Problem of Unemployment in the Commonwealth Caribbean", in Singham A.W. (editor): *The Commonwealth Caribbean in the Seventies*, 1975, pp. 1–15
11. Opening Statement at the 2nd Meeting of the Conference of Heads of Government of the Caribbean Community, December 8, 1975
12. Opening Remarks at 8th Meeting of the Common Market Council of Ministers, St George's, Grenada, April 23, 1976
13. "Independence and Development in the Leeward and Windward Islands", Royal Commonwealth Society, London, UK 1976.
14. "The Role of the Economic Integration Process in Regional Development: The Caribbean Experience", Institute of Latin American Studies, University of London, December 14, 1976
15. "Towards a New International Economic Order": Commonwealth Expert Group, Commonwealth Secretariat, 1977
16. "The Current State of International Commodity Negotiations", in G. Goodwin and J. Mayall (eds.): A New International Commodity Regime, (London, Croom Helm, 1979)
17. "National Development: Aspects of the Task Ahead" – Address to UWI Graduates, February 9, 1980

18. "Adjustments of the Caribbean Economies to Changing International Economic Relations", Opening Statement to the 16th West Indian Agricultural Economics Conference, 1982

19. Statement at Panel on South-South Cooperation. SID World Conference July 21, 1982

20. Statement on UNCTAD VI at the 9th Annual European General Assembly of Non-Governmental Organizations for Development, Contact with European Communities, Brussels April 12, 1983

21. Centre for World Development Education – London, Statement – May 3, 1983

22. "Review of Integration Movements in the Third World with Particular Reference to the Caribbean Community", Symposium of Ten Years of CARICOM Integration Experience, Barbados, July 4, 1983

23. "The Caribbean After Grenada: Four challenges Facing the Regional Movement", May 1984

24. "South-South Trade: A growing dimension of UNCTAD's work" Twentieth Anniversary Special Issue, UNCTAD Bulletin, No. 205, September 1984

25. "The Role of Trade in the Economic Reactivation Process in Latin America and the Caribbean", Statement at UNDP Regional Meeting, Santo Domingo, November 12, 1984

26. "Development Co-operation after UNCTAD VI: Aspects of the Intellectual Task Ahead", Institute of Development Studies, Bulletin, Vol. 15, No. 3, 1984

27. "South-South Trade and Economic Co-operation, Notes on Future Strategy", South-South II, Kuala Lumpur, Malaysia, 1986

28. "UNCTAD at Work" (with Marcial Plehn-Mejia, May 1987)

29. "Marketing of Commodities: Approaches and Arrangements for Developing Countries" July 1986, Seminar on Commodities, Ministry of Primary Commodities, Kuala Lumpur, Malaysia

30. "The International Economic Situation: Elements for a Policy Agenda" – Keynote Address – First Association of Caribbean Economists Conference, Mona, July 1987

31. Address at the 25th Anniversary of the Bank of Jamaica 1987

32. "The West Indian University Re-Visited" – 6th Dr Eric Williams Memorial Lecture, Trinidad, June 18, 1988

33. "Caribbean Visions: A Tribute to Sir Arthur Lewis", in Sir Arthur Lewis, 1989. Barbados: Caribbean Studies Association, XIV Annual Conference, May 23, 1989.

34. "The Right to Choose; Some Lessons of Independence in the Field of External Economic Relations", Castries, St Lucia, September 1989

35. "The Importance of Productivity Growth in the Caribbean", Address to the Caribbean Association of Industry and Commerce Awards Banquet, Guadeloupe, May 26, 1989

36. "Exchange Rate and Tariff Policies: A Brief Commentary", CDB/ILPES Senior Policy Seminar, Barbados, May 22–24, 1989

37. "Education in the West Indies" – Address to CIDA, November 1989

areas in which the University of the West Indies (UWI) can work with you, and this is the essential purpose of the Roundtable.

It seeks to provide a forum where business and the University can put their heads together and address critical practical issues of today and tomorrow and see what we can do together to improve the business climate and business capacity for the new age.

Let me tell you what the UWI is already doing, thanks to the support of external donors – especially USAID and many of the companies represented here today. Our Institute of Business is growing fast, both in capacity and in the range of services being provided. We have trained about 20 members of faculty at the master's level and have 10 in training at the doctoral level, 5 of whom will return next year. We hope to continue increasing the number of doctorates over the next few years. We are recruiting senior faculty to add to those already on the ground and have arrangements with leading institutions to provide us with visiting faculty.

Our Executive Master of Business Administration (EMBA) programme is now well established, and our regular Master of Business Administration (MBA) programme will be in place by next year.

We have a continuing programme of specialized short courses and a more general executive development programme. We are ready to mount custom-tailored courses to fit the needs of individual companies or groups.

Research and consulting services are also available and are already being utilized by some companies and the Government of Jamaica. We are in the process of establishing a collaborative programme of joint master's degrees with three universities in the Dominican Republic.

These programmes will be bilingual and will involve our students doing internships in business and government in the Spanish-speaking Caribbean. Among the areas directly relevant to business are the programmes in international business, economic development and reform, agricultural diversification, and natural resources management.

This is also a critical step forward in making Spanish the second language of our institution. If we succeed, we shall be providing you in the period ahead with bilingual graduates who can staff operations which you may wish to establish in the rest of the Caribbean and Latin America.

As part of this programme, we intend to plan a series of workshops and seminars for other business sectors so that knowledge of and contacts with businesspersons in other parts of the Caribbean can grow.

This is one strand of a general strategy that we are developing. We are building partnerships and networks with academic institutions in other parts of the world. Higher education is one of the sectors which is becoming globalized at a rapid rate.

Universities should aim to be competitive with the best institutions worldwide. This is leading to mergers among small institutions, consortia, networks, team-teaching, educational franchising and other forms of collaboration.

These arrangements are permitting institutions to exploit their comparative advantages and to correct weaknesses in their own capacity.

I give one example. We have recently been invited to join a worldwide network of six leading medical schools. In the United Kingdom, three prestigious schools – Guys, St Thomas' and Kings – have merged into a single entity. They have invited us to join a contribute towards that end. It is hoped that the Ministers of Trade in the region could be encouraged to take the necessary steps towards a combined effort of investigation in order to develop proposals for taking this matter forward in the inter-governmental machinery.

In looking towards the future, it is important to notice the initiatives already in place by some governments and institutions in developing trade and supportive relations with China. This has so far been focused on infrastructural development, but presumably the next stage would include greater attention to the growth of economic and financial relations. The Chinese economy can be a major market for Caribbean niche products and also services, a major one of which is tourism.

The foregoing commentary in this epilogue would be incomplete without a full acknowledgement of the invaluable part played by the four editors in conceiving of the entire volume and bringing it to fruition. They deserve every commendation for their efforts, insight and dedication.

38. "Human Resource Development; Its Relevance to Jamaica and the Caribbean" – Grace Kennedy Foundation Lecture, 1990

39. "The Caribbean After 1992" – Sir Thomas Holland Memorial Lecture, Royal Society of Arts, London, UK April 24, 1990

40. "New Directions in Education in the OECS Countries", Education Conference, St Lucia, May 20, 1990

41. "The European Single Market: The Need for Vigilance and Innovation by CARICOM Countries", May 24, 1990

42. "Aspects of the External Environment for Caribbean Growth and Development in the 1990s" – May 1990

43. "Issues in the International Economy" – 1st Annual CEO Seminar, IOB, St Augustine, June 9, 1990

44. "Preparing for 1992", Statement to the West India Committee Conference on Europe & the Caribbean, November 20, 1990

45. Opening Remarks – Discussion at Harvard Business Club, January 10, 1991

46. Address to the Joint Annual Human Resource Development Programme, Progress Review with the World Bank, Jamaica, February 1991

47. "The Global Economy" – Re-Thinking Development, Consortium Graduate School of the Social Sciences, April 1991

48. "Globalization and Identity – The Dual Challenge" – June 24, 1991

49. "Confronting the Challenges of Change" – Annual Address to the UWI Community – September 1991

50. "The Future of CARICOM in the Global Economy", PIOJ Symposium, Jamaica, October 6, 1991

51. "Planning Social Change" – Panel Discussion, October 26, 1991

52. "Long Term Changes in Europe/Caribbean Relations: Some Potential Areas for Co-operation", November 20, 1991

53. "Deficiencies in Education Thwarting Regional Development", Article published in the "The Gleaner", March 8, 1992

54. Launch of the UWI Press – Address, April 24, 1992

55. "Opening our Windows to the World", Address to the UWI Community, Academic Year 1992

56. "Address to the Opening of the UWI Alumni Conference-Unlocking the Potential of a Region", April 15, 1993

57. "Trends in the International Business Environment: Guidelines for the Caribbean Private Sector", June 19, 1993, Castries, St Lucia

58. Annual Address to the UWI Community, at the start of the Academic Year, September 1993

59. "The Second Period of Lomé IV; Its Implications for the Post Lomé Era", Address to the Sixth Europe/Caribbean Conference in Santo Domingo, DR, 1993

60. "Some General Issues of Governance" – Inaugural Meeting of the Commission on Governance, Council Room, Mona, November 1, 1993

61. Address – Annual Awards Ceremony Jamaica Chamber of Commerce, Pegasus Hotel, February 4, 1994

62. Economic and Social Development and Global Governance – Chap. 5 – Commission on Global Governance, April 8, 1994

63. "The Survival of Small States in a Changing International Environment", MFA, T & T, June 17, 1994

64. "The Importance of Negotiation Preparedness: Reflections on the Caribbean Experience", Dialogue – A Policy Bulletin of Caribbean Affairs, No. 1 July/ August 1994

65. "Leadership: Responding to the Needs of Our Time": IBM Leadership Banquet, September 8, 1994

66. "Issues in Human Resource Development" – A Commentary Paper for the World Bank, 1995

67. Partners in Education, Statement delivered at CHIC '95, San Juan, Puerto Rico, June 12, 1995

68. Basic Education Reform Project, Castries, St Lucia, Opening Statement, August 13, 1995

69. "Education and Training – The Keys to Survival of Developing Countries" – 9th World Conference on Cooperative Education, Jamaica Pegasus Hotel, August 31, 1995

70. Conference on Prospects for Services Exports in the Caribbean, Rose Hall May 13–14, 1995 – Welcoming Remarks

71. Challenges to Jamaica and the Role of the Business Roundtable – First Annual Vice Chancellor's Business Roundtable, Mona Campus, September 15, 1995

72. "Challenges Facing the UWI for the 21st Century", October 7, 1995

73. "Some Personal Reflections" Towards a Caribbean Economy in the Twenty-first Century: Essays in Honour of William G Demas, L Clarke and M G Zephrin (eds): CCMS, 1997, pp.13–17

74. "Overcoming Obstacles and Maximizing Opportunities": A Report by the Independent Group of Experts on Smaller Economies and the Western Hemisphere Integration, 1997

75. "Negotiating the Export Economy", The Third Sir Arthur Lewis Memorial Lecture St George's, Grenada, November 4, 1998

76. "Changing Perceptions of Development: Their Implications for the Caribbean" – Inaugural William Demas Memorial Lecture, Barbados, October 11, 2000

77. "Challenges Facing Caribbean Integration" – INTAL Forum, Buenos Aires, November 2000

78. Statement on Finance and Development – OECS, January 24, 2002

79. Speaking Notes – Opening of Sir Alister McIntyre Building, UWI, Mona, September 2, 2002

80. "The Imperatives for Economic Growth in the OECS", November 2002

81. The Cotonou Agreement – Speaking Notes – First Eleven Briefing Room, January 31, 2003

82. Regional Trade Agreements: Speaking Notes, June 15, 2003

83. "The Meaning of the CARICOM Single Market and Economy", June 29, 2003 – Speaking Notes

84. "Lloyd Best: Reminiscences of the Early Days" in S. Ryan (ed): Independent Thought and Caribbean Freedom: Essays in Honour of Lloyd Best (SALISES, St Augustine, 2003, pp. 389–396)
85. International Trade and Cooperation for Development: Some Contemporary Challenges – Rough Notes
86. International Economic Relations – Speaking Notes, 2003
87. "International Trade Negotiations" – April 19, 2004
88. "Striving for Excellence", Address to Faculty of Social Science Students, UWI, Mona, March 18, 2004
89. CARICOM Trade Policy, Speaking Points – July 2, 2004
90. Mona Academic Conference, Speaking Points – August 27, 2004
91. "Increasing the Contribution of Tourism to Jamaica's Development" – Closing Remarks at the Final Session of UWI Mona Academic Conference, August 28, 2005
92. "International Competitiveness and Caribbean Development" – Launch of the Competitiveness Company, September 20, 2005
93. "Reviewing the position of the OECS as Less Developed Countries in CARICOM", October 2, 2005
94. "Productivity and Efficiency Issues in UWI": Some Working Notes – Regional Symposium on Tertiary Education Financing, Barbados, November 21–24, 2005
95. Understanding Caribbean Children – Opening Remarks at Caribbean Child Research Conference, UWI, Mona, October 26, 2006
96. "The Knowledge Economy" – Dr Eric Williams Memorial lecture, May 2006
97. "Small Countries in the World Economy: Some Observations Relevant to the Caribbean", September 2006
98. "International Trade and Cooperation for Development: Some Contemporary Challenges" – Rough Notes – November 2007
99. Governance and Decentralization in the Context of the Regional University, Notes – March 7, 2008
100. "Caribbean Integration and Development: Some Further Steps Re-Conceptualizing Integration for Development", March 27, 2008
101. "The Conference on Policies and Strategies to Face the Global Downturn", Statement – Bridgetown, Barbados, October 16, 2009
102. Address on the Occasion of the Opening of the Alister McIntyre Building – Cave Hill Campus, Barbados, October 2009